SURVIVOR OF A
TARNISHED MINISTRY

The True Story of Mike and Betty Esses

By
Betty Esses DeBlase

Santa Ana, California

If you have any counseling requests or comments, direct your inquires to:

Betty Esses DeBlase
P.O. Box 3585
Orange, CA 92665

Truth Publishers
Santa Ana, California 92705

ISBN 0-913621-00-5

To
My loving husband, Bob, who gave me back my life
again...and put me on a pedestal.

To
My children, who with me, survived the storm.

And to my grandchild,
Danielle, who is the reason for this book.

Contents

Preface

How can I lay my life out on paper for everyone to look at? How do I admit my part in the pretense, the sham, the out-right lies that were a large part of our marriage and ministry. And having admitted the lies and sins in Mike's life and also my own, how can I show that God *has* taught me through this, that I *am* recovering at long last, that I am *now* clean before the Lord, and that my Savior *wants* to use Mike's and my story for the glory of his kingdom?

Oh, it's not hard just remembering and recounting all that happened over those twenty-eight years. The emotional investment in those years can bring it all back to me almost instantly—as clearly as when it all happened. The pain, the love, the sorrow, the joy, the anger, the forgiveness, the frustration, the peace. And most of it mixed up, jumbled together, a confusion of divided loyalties and naive compromise. No, it's not hard to remember. It's hard to face. But as hard as all that is to face, it is impossible for me now, after I have experienced the blessed forgiveness of Jesus Christ and renewal by the Holy Spirit, to continue with perpetuating the deception. Telling the truth is not easy. Not telling the truth is impossible.

Mike's and my stories were told before. (Mike's in *Michael, Michael, Why Do You Hate Me?*, and mine in *If I Can, You Can*.) But what was told before was a mixture of gospel truth and human deception. As you will see in the following pages, Mike's true story was far different from his book. And while I was giving the secrets for a successful Christian marriage in my book, I was unable to cope with my own marriage, which rapidly was falling apart. And yet Mike and I were not unique. There are hundreds of Christian leaders around the world whose personal and family lives have many more problems than they would ever admit or reveal in public. The popular saying is, "Christians aren't perfect, just forgiven." That's not an excuse for sin, but it is an observation on our fallible condition, which will be perfected only in the resurrection.

Contrary to what many Christians glibly spout, it is not easy to live the Christian life. Living a life consistently submitted to Jesus Christ takes a lot of dedication, a lot of hard work, and a lot of humility. And if it weren't for the abundant grace of God, our best efforts would even fail. The old hymn *Amazing Grace* is right when it points out that it's grace that brings us through adversity. We can't rest on grace, though, expecting that we'll sail along, sinless, just by not doing anything. That's a vicious trap, and one of the quickest ways I know to fall into compromise. This true story of the failure of a marriage and the failure of a ministry is not meant to teach defeatism; it's meant to be a goad to push us into *acting* on our commitments, into actively *grabbing* God's grace, and into *diligently* submitting *every facet* of our lives to the Lordship of Jesus Christ.

If I didn't have the assurance of God's forgiveness and the knowledge that God can use all things—even Mike's and my shortcomings—to bring him praise, I wouldn't be writing this book. I dont want to go over what is past. I don't want to disillusion those who trusted us. I don't want to sound like the bitter ex-wife. I don't want to act holier-than-thou. But God's way is not always the easy way and I *know* he wants the true story told. Over the last several years the Lord has been showing me how he is going to use this negative story for *positive* good.

First, simply confessing my own failures to my brothers and sisters in Christ is healthy for me, both spiritually and emotionally, as much as it hurts. Second, I know there are dozens of women in Christian ministry who feel trapped just like I did and who need to know that it is possible to escape from the trap of deceit. They think no one knows how they feel, no one knows what's really going on, and no one can help them. Jesus Christ does know how they feel, and he's the only one with real help. I'm not saying the answers are always easy, but without Jesus Christ, there are *no* answers. Third, this story will serve as a warning to those who support Christian ministries and those who may be called into Christian ministry. Just because someone says he's called by God and looks and sounds good, that doesn't mean he's already been perfected and he never sins! Christians, don't be satisfied with compromise and mediocrity in your own lives or in the lives of your shepherds. Recognizing we are fallible is no excuse for rampant sin and disobedience, especially at the expense of our Lord's honor and the trust of God's people. Fourth, God will use this story to give some Christians the proper perspective regarding his servants, the leaders of our churches.

If you are familiar with the "wonderful spirit-filled Esses ministry" of years gone by, and you looked to Mike or me as nearly perfect, you'll be shocked by what you read here. But God will take that shock and show you that you may have been guilty of "idol worship." If you look to others for God, you'll end up being exploited, shocked, and disappointed. But if you look to Jesus Christ himself, the God-man, you will be eternally blessed, constantly reassured, and never disappointed. Fifth and finally, this true story is an exhortation to excellence in Christian commitment. Don't settle for a life that's Christian in little more than name. Don't settle for a ministry that can't be distinguished from the hard sell games of the world. With the grace and power of God we *can* do better!

Jesus is the one who knows our hearts. He knows when the desire of our hearts is to serve him honestly, even when we sometimes fall on our faces and feel trapped by circumstances and actions we know are wrong. He just wants us to pick ourselves up, brush ourselves off, and start all over again. The problems are overwhelming only when we try to fool ourselves, those around us, and even our Lord. Then we are in grave danger of being unable ever to rise from the ground. That's when we have no hope of ever getting up again.

My prayer is that God will use my life to set some prisoners free, to enable other marriages to be healed with the light of truth, and to protect the innocent sheep who sit in thousands of pews every Sunday and are so easily fleeced. Revenge is bitter. Truth is liberating.

CHAPTER 1

Why Isn't Daddy Here?

It has come at last, the task I have been avoiding with the frantic desperation of a mouse shrinking from a hungry cat. I've tried every crack and crevice for cover, to no avail. I've screamed above the roar of the waves at the seashore and I've whispered into my pillow at night, "I don't want to tell this story." Yet, the Hound of Heaven has never lost my scent for a minute. Each time I have shouted "NO!", he has whispered "yes." Each time I find another excuse for covering up the past, he has made the same challenge: to tell the truth.

As we drove home, leaving my dear Laurie and my new grand-daughter in the hospital, we watched the street lights slowly dim and vanish as the first faint rays of the morning sun began to streak across the sky. I turned to my husband of a little over a year, Bob, with tears on my cheeks, resignation in my eyes. "Bob, I'm going to have to tell the whole story. The Lord isn't going to let me off the hook." Bob's hands gripped the wheel even tighter, like he was clutching a life preserver. He knew what this would do to us. He voiced what I had been telling myself: "Are you sure, Betty Lee? You know they'll eat you up alive. No one really wants to know the truth."

Gazing out the window, I thought for a minute before I answered him. "Honey, tonight waiting for the baby to be born, I knew that I couldn't deny the Lord any longer. All those hours of worry over Laurie and her child tore down the last of my defenses. You know all of my excuses, you've heard them often enough, but after tonight they just don't matter. Jesus said he is the truth. How can Laurie trust Jesus when she can't even trust her own father who claims to serve in his Name? As long as I cover up in front of the world what Mike did to perpetuate a lie in the name of Jesus, I can't face Laurie honestly. She knows Jesus and she knows Mike. As long as I'm silent and not faithful to the truth, I can't ask her to be faithful."

My eyes returned to the window, and I heaved a great sigh of acceptance, a reluctant sigh, but still a sigh of acceptance. My thoughts returned to my courageous daughter. I had just left her— exhausted but ecstatic, Laurie, a new mother. I guess my defense crumbled when my daughter came through our bedroom door early that night. One look at her white face and the first crack in the dam I'd been building so laboriously began to appear. I would have done anything to take away the labor pain. Another crack showed up on the way to the hospital when, out of shelter of the circle of my arms, I heard the small, hurting voice of my child whisper, "Oh Mom, why isn't Daddy here?"

Why isn't Daddy here? That's a question any Mother should be able to answer her child, but it isn't one I can answer. I don't know why her Daddy isn't here, and I probably never will know.

I tried to give Laurie a "Christian World." I've taught her from birth about the love of Jesus. Laurie has learned her lessons well. She loves the Lord with all her heart and soul. She is a shining example of a Christian in the finest sense of the word.

And yet, her Christian world has been marred over the years. She's been through so much. Laurie: my youngest, yet my oldest, the one I've turned to for solace and comfort over the years. Laurie: as lovely inside as she is outside. Oh my Laurie, how do I erase from your mind the hurts and pain that have come your way, not because you deserved them, but because of who you are, the daughter of Michael and Betty Esses?

The Christian Body is sick. It is sick with unforgiveness. It is sick with corruption. It is sick with erroneous teaching, or no teaching. It is sick with idol worship: man worshipping man, not man worshipping God. It is sick with pride and inflated egos that eclipse men with their ravenous needs to be fed with adoration and unthinking, unquestioning loyalty.

Back at home I was too tense to sleep, but lay rigid on the bed, not wanting to bother Bob, but haunted by the past and its effect on the night's events. No, tonight's events have proved too much for me to seek the sweet refuge of sleep. I feel such a desperate need for answers I can rely on, facts that I can point to and say, "This is why all these things happened."

Even though dawn is breaking and I have been up all night, my body no longer yearns for the oblivion of sleep that I have sought on so many other nights. I'm intent upon the decision I have made: Revelation, everything revealed, my life laid open for everyone to see. All the rocks turned over. All the skeletons chased from all the closets. All the drawers emptied and cleaned, and all the dust kittens out from under the bed. To me this has been a momentous decision. It goes against everything I have been doing most of my life.

The old ways were so easy to slip into. Cover, hide the truth, pretend it never happened, rationalize, make excuses, keep up a front, don't lose face, don't disillusion the people, don't hurt the body of believers These are some of the maxims by which I once lived. These were rocks on which I once stood. Now the Lord is taking them out from under me, saying, "My people need to hear the truth. My people will be healed only with the truth. My people will grow only with the truth. My people will be protected only with the truth."

I know now that I can't keep still any longer. I don't want to hand my little granddaughter the same world I gave her mother, a world of half-truths, evasions, and pain. I want to give her every good thing that a child of God deserves. I'm not talking about the "rose garden" some people expect when they become Christians. I know, and I have taught, that we can expect the trials and tribulations that help us grow and help make us the men and women God wants us to be. But we do need to be able to enjoy a spiritually healthy climate in which to grow.

The cancer that has invaded the Christian world is growing stronger all the time. Its tentacles are wrapped around the business ethics of the church, the scruples of its leaders, the morals of its shepherds, and the lives of its sheep. The only way to eradicate it is with the healing laser of truth.

Laser! That's the word, the concept for which I've been searching. A laser beam is so narrow and intense it concentrates and destroys only the unhealthy tissue. Oh God, give me your wisdom to bring a beam of truth to your people, destroying that which is rotten, all that unhealthy tissue that your people are stumbling over, some never to rise again. Yet Lord, make this beam so narrow that it will leave that which is good, clean, and enduring totally unscathed.

I've seen so many of the Lord's people, including myself, bogged down in the mire, not always of our creation, but the result of misplaced loyalties, hero worship, and being led with the myopic eyes of lambs to the slaughter. Jesus, open our eyes, give us the mind to accept truth as the healing agent it is and hearts to accept the love your surgery brings.

I listen to the soft, even breathing of my husband. The darkness around me becomes transparent, a screen upon which my life unfolds, illuminated by my desperate need to remember, to weigh everything that happened, the good and the bad. Slowly the blurred images on the screen take form and they become a young man and a younger woman, but unmistakably Michael and Betty Esses on the day of their wedding. It's not a joyous story, but it's a true story and a story that can heal, exhort, and protect.

CHAPTER 2

From The Beginning

I was starting to be lulled into oblivion by the purr of the car as it traveled through the starless night, taking me farther and farther away from my family. The panic that had flowed through my body for the last few hours was beginning to ebb a little, and a semblance of reason began to tip-toe across my mind.

With eyes squeezed tightly closed so the man beside me would not be aware that sleep had not yet overtaken me, I tried to assess what had happened that placed me in this position. I was in a car I didn't want to be in, traveling to a place I didn't want to go to, with a man who was to be my husband, but who was still in many ways a stranger to me.

I had met with Mike (a nickname, his real name was Max) Esses the night before, having every intention of breaking off my relationship with him completely. My parents had finally convinced me that marriage to Michael had about as much chance as the proverbial "snowball in hell."

Michael was nearly nine years older than I. He had been married and had fathered four children, and I was barely 18 years old. It wasn't until later that I found out he wasn't divorced yet when we married. After his divorce, we remarried, just to set things straight. My father said, as he tried to reason with me, "Betty Lee, this man has already lived a lifetime, and you're just beginning to live."

There were other things that my folks felt doomed the relationship. Mike was an Arabic Jew and an atheist, while I was raised in a typical WASP (white Anglo-Saxon Protestant) family. Mike was a first-generation American, from a culture that was basically Arabic. Even the music was Arabic. My people were so

American we often joked that our ancestors came over on the Mayflower.

My background was middle class, grass-roots American, New Mexico, Texas-based. Mine was a world of country clubs, golf tournaments, football games, and barbecues. My parents had no hope that our two backgrounds could produce a harmonious marriage.

But I had fallen in love with Mike, who was so much more experienced than I. Mike had the ability to charm the birds out of the trees, and even though Mike's charms were lost on my mother and father, they were not lost on me. My head could tell me what was right, but my heart followed Mike everywhere he led. The night I was going to break up with Mike was a case in point. Before I knew it, I had abandoned my decision and agreed to run away with him and get married.

On the way in the car the distance separating me from my folks and their love and protection seemed like a million miles away. Mike's charm and my own youthfull rebellion together started me on my twenty-eight year mistake. My decision would haunt me later, when I would rail against God for giving me such a difficult and contradictory husband, and then realize I hadn't sought his opinion on Mike in the beginning and so was hardly in a position to complain about my own rebellious choice later on.

It didn't take very long for the fruit of my rebellion to ripen. A problem that plagued our marriage consistently through the years reared its ugly head the first year we were married. Mike's first adultery during our marriage stabbed at my heart and nearly destroyed me emotionally. I had no warning and didn't even think that the circumstances necessitating our two weddings could have been a warning of the pattern that would run throughout our marriage.

We were living in Portland, Oregon. Michael was employed by Eastern Department Store as a buyer for children's wear. We had begun to make some friends, and after a short time we began to see one particular couple quite often. The husband was a police officer, and a fine man. I had a hard time getting close to the wife, but chalked it up to the fact that I was so much younger than she was and so we really didn't have much in common. It didn't make much difference because Mike liked both of them so well that we always had fun with them.

After a few months our fun began unravelling. Every time I called Mike at work he was out of the store. He told me that he had to be out because he was looking at the lines of different salesmen who showed their products at their hotels.

I wasn't suspicious at all because Mike's explanation made sense, but Geneva's husband was not as gullible as I. He investigated some of her stories and the roof fell in on all of us. Mike and Geneva were meeting at different hotels in town.But they weren't always alone. One of her girlfriends joined them and made it a threesome.

When I found out, I thought I was going to die. I loved Mike so much, he had become practically the air that I breathed. Nothing in my life had prepared me for this. My father had never looked at another woman during his marriage, and he was the only male role model I had. It had never occurred to me that once I was married I would ever have to contend with an unfaithful husband.

Later in my years of counseling women, I came face to face with this agony in other wives many times. It comes in different stages...disbelief...anger...the feeling of betrayal...the anguish of trying to accept what has happened...self-recrimination (if only I had done something different)...and, last but not least, the attempt to set your heartache aside by forgiving.

Forgiveness is ultimately your only option, but each time you still go through all of the other stages first. Even with complete forgiveness, something is lost from the marriage that can never be replaced. You can never look at your mate again and know they have kept themselves only for you, "till death do you part."

I had fought my parents so aggressively in order to marry Mike that I just couldn't admit defeat. Against all their objections I had maintained that I was an adult, wise enough to have found a beautiful jewel under Michael's rough surface. In order to get out of my marriage, I would have to confess that I had been wrong.

For nearly two years I had extolled this man's virtues to the skies. I had bragged of his sincerity, and of his deep and abiding love for me. I had blown up every kindness extended to me into proof of Michael's "sainthood." In short, I did everything a child does to get his own way. Now I was stuck with the fruit of my rebellion and pride.

I recognize this behavior now that I have raised children of my own. A child does not realize that when something is right and good it needs very little defense. Every time my children have gone into a high-pressure sales pitch to get me to "buy" their latest notion, my parental antenna goes up a mile. I am well aware that you have to say very little about pure gold to authenticate it, but selling "fool's gold" takes a super salesman.

Geneva's husband terminated his wife's game abruptly by confronting her. Thus began and ended the first of the string of affairs that I lived through all the years of my marriage.

CHAPTER 3

On The Run

I don't know if it had anything to do with Geneva's husband being a policeman, but shortly after the exposure of his affair, Michael came down with a recurrence of the rheumatic fever he had suffered with as a child. He didn't seem sick, but he said he could no longer tolerate the rainy climate of Portland.

I didn't want to leave my family and travel all the way to the east coast. But the knowledge that I would be three thousand miles from Geneva was enough to erase any doubts from my mind. What I didn't realize then was that no matter where we went it would be only a matter of time before the next affair would come along.

The first place we headed was Miami, Florida. Mike's brother lived there with his wife and children. His father also made his home with his brother, and Mike was anxious to see him. It had been quite a few years since Mike had left his father in New York. The relationship with his family had been strained because his first wife had been an Italian—not the expected Jewish girl.

Mike at first tried to pass me off as a Jewish girl to his father. The man was quite old and completely blind, so I guess Michael thought he could keep the peace this way. The only thing he hadn't counted on was how sharp his father was. The very first night when we sat down at the supper table I inadvertently gave the whole thing away. I had no idea that according to Jewish dietary law you couldn't mix dairy products with meat. We were having lamb for the main course and when I asked for a glass of milk to drink, the jig was up.

But even though I wasn't Jewish, Mike's father was very kind to me and would admonish his son to take good care of me. I felt awful the day he died and Mike was away at the race track instead of with his critically ill father.

After Miami we headed for Scranton, Pennsylvania. Mike and his brothers opened a series of stores, and each brother became responsible for one. Even I was running a store in Scranton, while Mike had charge of one a few miles away in Wilkes-Barre.

Things ran smoothly for awhile until Mike started coming home later and later. Finally he began to stay out all night. It hurt just as much as the first time. I was sure he was having another affair. All speculation was laid to rest one night when he brought her home with him to help him move out.

I completely snapped. I got in our car and started driving to New York City. All I could think was that I had to get to Mike's brother Eddie and his wife. They had been like family to me. Speeding through the Pocono Mountains at over 100 miles per hour brought me to the attention of the highway patrol, and I was pulled over before I had gotten too far. I will never forget that patrolman. When he saw the condition I was in, he took me right home to his wife, who put me to bed and sat with me all night. I know those people saved my life. I never would have made some of those hairpin turns that were in those mountains. I didn't know the Lord yet, but I know he knew me and was already taking care of me.

When I arrived in New York City the next day, Eddie took one look at me and left for Scranton and Mike. I still don't know what he said to him, but Mike was in New York the next day begging me to come home. Once again I forgave him and we were back together again. But the hurt was not completely gone.

We moved to Philadelphia. This time it took six months for Michael to get involved again with another woman. I had had it. I called my mother and father and asked them to come and get me. The hours before I made that decision still stand out in my mind.

I had taken the gun Mike kept in his nightstand. Because of the pain and agony of once again being rejected, all I could think of was, "this is a quick way out of my misery." I put the gun to my head and pulled the trigger. At that moment the little dog I had bought just a few months before jumped on me, spoiling my aim so that the bullet went into the wall. I dropped to the floor and hugged that pup till she yelped.

At that moment, although I didn't know the Lord, he provided me with a reason to live. It wasn't much—not like my faith in the Lord or my love for my children, both of which sustained me through later years. But at this moment Jesus took care of me by using the trusting and beautiful eyes of my little puppy. I sat on the floor, holding that scared little mutt, thinking about what might have happened to her if I had succeeded in killing myself. I hadn't seen anyone for days. Mike was gone. I had no idea how long it would have been before someone would have found my body. The thought of a starving little dog, locked in a room with a corpse, made me think again about what I had tried to do. I don't know how long I sat there, but when I got up, I knew I would never be driven that far again.

I know that many readers will know exactly how I felt that day. You feel like it just hurts too much to take another breath or think another thought and so you just decide to quit. Many people are alone like I was. There is no one to talk to and you are unable to get any perspective on your situation.

Thirty years ago when I sat in that room and lifted that gun to my head there weren't any help lines or crisis centers. There weren't any shelters for desperate people. Now crisis counselors are as close as the telephone. Trained counselors can give you their shoulders, cry with you, advise you, give you someone to hang on to until it becomes bearable once more. I didn't have anyone. Now any telephone operator can connect anyone in a position like I was in with people who can help. I thank God for the help that's there now, and I thank God for the little dog who saved me so long ago.

It was a few hours later that I called my folks and asked them to come and get me. When I heard my dad and mother say, "We'll be out there as fast as we can get there," I was so grateful to God for giving me such wonderful parents. As disappointed as they were in my choice of Michael for a husband, they never caused us any trouble once the marriage was a fact. Michael admitted that he never had any in-law problems.

My father told me to get busy and sell my furniture so that I would be ready to go as soon as they could make the drive from the west coast. I put an ad in the paper and in a few days I was sleeping on the floor because there was nothing left in the house but packed boxes that we would haul back to California, my little puppy Amber, and me.

I made a pallet on the floor out of blankets to sleep on at night with Amber curled next to me. One morning I awakened to find Michael standing over me. He started shouting. "What have you done? Where is all our furniture? What in the hell is going on here?" With all the courage I could muster I told him to shut up and I'd tell him what I'd done. I told him that since I hadn't heard from him for a couple of weeks I had assumed he was gone for good. I said the furniture was sold and my parents were on their way to get me.

Michael didn't know what to say or do. He had come home to make up with me and I had already wrapped up our marriage in a neat little bundle and was prepared to dump it in the nearest trash can. Michael knew now that I had been pushed too far. He tried desperately to win me back with all the promises any girl could ever want to hear. Every declaration of love known to man spilled out of his mouth, along with total repentance for the disgraceful manner in which he had treated me.

Even though I knew Mike could be lying, I wanted to believe him so much. Believing is less painful than facing the truth. The truth is pretty brutal, for it tells you that you are perfectly capable of loving a man who thinks nothing of being unfaithful to you. This in turn causes you to lose respect for yourself and all semblance of self-esteem goes out the window. It becomes easier to believe him than to face the truth.

I relented—with one condition: I was still going to move back to California when my folks arrived, but I would let Mike come if he wanted to. Without a moment's hesitation Michael agreed.

Years later I found out why Mike capitulated so easily. My sister-in-law Gloria told me that the girl he had been involved with was Italian and a married woman. When her husband and her brothers found out about Michael they were furious. Gloria said the girl's family turned the city upside down looking for Mike, vowing all the time that if they caught up with him there would be nothing left but the pieces. She said Mike's brothers swore to the men that they had no idea where he had gone. My California move was just what Mike needed.

CHAPTER 4

The Calm In The Storm

After the upheavals and tears of the first years of my marriage, I didn't know what to expect in California. I steeled myself for more of the same. I wanted to forgive Mike and hope for the best for our future and that's what I honestly determined to do. But without even really thinking about it, I was holding my breath to see what would happen next.

When we arrived in California, we found a little apartment in Santa Monica. It was close to the beach and close to the sprawl of urban Los Angeles. The beach provided our recreation and Los Angeles provided Mike's first California job opportunity, as the manager of the parking lot and valet service at an exclusive restaurant.

Our small housewarming in Santa Monica marked the begining of what I call my "real marriage." These were the good years sandwiched between the years of anguish behind me and the years of agony in front of me. They consisted of about ten years in all, and in many ways they made the ultimate failure of our marriage so much more of a tragedy than if they never existed. They are now the faded memories of what could have been.

When I look back on our marriage as a whole I can't figure out why those ten years happened. They were like the calm in the middle of a storm. During those ten years I was happier with Mike than I thought possible, and after they were over I was more devastated than I ever could have imagined. One explanation I can think of is that Mike had been so afraid of the Italian familiy's threats before we left Philadelphia that he tried to be a normal, loving husband to me instead of risking being killed by some "conquest's" irate husband and family.

The only problem with getting your act together out of fear is that with time the memory of your close call fades and the fear fades along with it. You become willing once again to gamble on not getting caught. The only time a leopard really changes his spots is when he ceases to be a leopard anymore. True repentance and acceptance of the Lord causes the "old man" to die and the "new man" to emerge (2 Corinthians 5:16,17). How I wish true repentance had been the reason for those happy years. If it had, they never would have ended.

Another reason for the happy years may have been Mike's changed attitude toward business. For the first time he really committed himself to making a big success of his new business. Later during the same ten year period he worked just as hard at our custom drapery business. The only drawback to managing the restaurant parking lots and valet services was that it took a seemingly endless number of hours to do the job well. Mike worked from 11 A.M. to 2 A.M., six and even sometimes seven days a week. The only way I could see him regularly was to go down to the lots to sit with him.

The restaurants catered to the well-known, the rich, and the "beautiful people." Some of the people I observed were, in fact, not so beautiful. I've seen movie stars I had admired on the screen so staggering drunk they could hardly walk to their cars. I used to pray as they drove out that no one would get in the way until they made it home.

One day Mike's brother Eddie, who also had moved his family to California, came to Michael and told him of a business in the nearby city of Anaheim that was available. Eddie knew how tired both Mike and I were of the long hours he was working and thought this business would be easier for us. It was a custom drapery business, and after we looked it over we decided to buy.

Both Mike and I worked in our new business and it brought us closer together than we had ever been. We were with each other twenty-four hours a day, but instead of getting on each other's nerves, we got along better than ever. We shared a feeling of accomplishment because we were making a very successful business out of one that had been failing. Our satisfaction turned to true joy on the unforgettable day I received news that I could hardly believe: I was pregnant. We had been married for ten years and finally I was pregnant. I can't express how wonderful this news was to me, because I had given up hoping for this miracle of life years before. The doctors had told me my chances of conceiving were almost nonexistent.

In fact, when the morning sickness began I thought something had gone wrong with my recovery from recent intestinal surgery. Pregnancy never occurred to me. I'll never forget lying on that examination table, complaining to the doctor about what he'd done to me in surgery. He started laughing and said, "Betty, I didn't do this to you! You're pregnant!"

My doctor was in Los Angeles and I had to wait through my thirty-mile drive back to Anaheim to give Mike the good news. To say he was happy would miss the mark completely. He started laughing and crying at the same time. As he held me in his arms, all I could think about was how happy I was that I hadn't let my marriage end back in Pennsylvania. Now we were a real family!

Those next few months while I was carrying my baby were the happiest of my life. Mike treated me like I was a fragile Dresden doll. My every wish was his command. I didn't have to ask for pickles and ice cream—he brought them before I even craved them.

I marveled at Mike's excitement and anticipation. Over the years he had acted like he didn't even care about having children. He had left four children behind from his first marriage that he never bothered with. I had always been the one agonizing over having my own child to hold. But Mike was at least as excited as I was.

My obstetrician had told me that this would probably be the only baby I would ever have, since it was quite unusual that I had gotten pregnant in the first place. Well, if I could only have one baby, I couldn't help wanting that baby to be a girl. I started making all my plans around a girl. Her room was painted pink. Her bassinet was pink and white checked gingham with white eyelet trim. Ballerinas danced across her walls and pink teddy bears were propped in the corners of her crib. I started making dresses of every pastel color, trimming them with lace and ribbons, ready for the little girl they would adorn. April of 1960 found our own Kathleen Joan Esses sleeping soundly in her nursery. Her room was festooned with pink and white balloons blown up by her daddy for her homecoming.

How can I express my pleasure in this little girl? She was the answer to my years of longing, the fulfillment of dreams I thought would never come true. Her daddy adored her and her mother never ceased to wonder at the miracle granted by a loving God. Kathy was the delight of our lives.

We are a family. These words danced in my head as I watched Mike bathe and diaper his little girl. When she developed colic her daddy would take her for long drives so the motion of the car would lull her to sleep. I would sit at the window of our home and watch our car go round and round the block, marveling at the difference I was seeing in my husband. This man, whom I knew was capable of being so mean and uncaring, was like putty in the hands of baby Kathy. Sometimes, when I look back at the times Michael rocked our baby in the rocking chair for hours, I can't help wondering. What might have happened in Mike's life if the future of this child had not been so suddenly and irrevocably changed?

If I could choose one day in my life to erase, I would not hesitate in my choice for one moment. It would be the day I took my beautiful, healthy baby to her pediatrician for her well-baby checkup and the first of her D.P.T. immunizations. Kathy and I must live with the sad results of this day for the rest of our lives.

Even with the new baby, I was still working with Mike in our drapery business, so after I left the doctor I went to the store and put Kathy to sleep in the crib we had for her there. It wasn't long before a strange noise coming from her crib brought Mike and me running. We found our little girl in the grip of a terrible convulsion. Mike and I rushed her back to the doctor's office. When we arrived Kathy was still convulsing. They worked with her there until they had her quiet again and then we had to put her into the hospital to determine what had happened. After many tests, including a painful spinal tap, they came to the conclusion that Kathy had had an anaphylactoid (hyper-sensitive) reaction to one of the drugs in the quadrigen making up her D.P.T. shot. Quadrigen was taken off the market about six months later, for causing erratic side effects.

The doctors didn't know how much effect, if any, this reaction would have on Kathy's future. They told us to take her home, watch her carefully, and keep her under close doctor's care. We did all these things. I moved her crib into our room in case something happened at night. I wouldn't even leave her room when she took a nap.

In a few months the doctor, Mike, and my parents all breathed a sigh of relief, for it seemed that the emergency was over, and Kathy was going to be all right. I was the only one who was still worried. I couldn't put my finger on it, I just knew something was wrong. She was progressing well. She was calling me Mama, and was standing up holding on to her crib when she was nine months old. All the books I was reading said this was normal development, yet alarm bells were going off in my head that no one else could hear. There was a shadow I saw in her eyes sometimes that would fill me with such sorrow that all I could do was sit and hold my baby and cry.

I would try to tell Mike how I felt, but he would just shrug it off as being the result of my new pregnancy. Much to the amazement of my doctor and me, two months after I gave birth to Kathy I was pregnant again. My two babies would be only eleven months apart.

In December Kathy was ten months old. We had decorated our Christmas tree, placed an angel on top, and piled gifts for our baby's first Christmas underneath the tree. Mike and I were relaxing on the couch, talking about the coming new baby, when once again those horrible sounds of convulsion filled the room. Kathy had gone into what was diagnosed later as status epilepsy (when there is one seizure after another). Mike couldn't believe his eyes. He had been so sure this would never happen again.

We frantically dialed her doctor and he said to rush her to the hospital as fast as possible. He would meet us there. When we got into the car I was holding a baby jerking in uncontrollable convulsions, but in a few minutes she got deathly still. I strained to hear her breathing. There was nothing. I started screaming at

Mike, "She's dead! She's dead! Our baby is dead!"

I really don't know what happened next. The world for me went blank. Mike told me later that when we arrived at the emergency room he got out of the car and tried to take Kathy away from me, but I wouldn't let go of her. He said I kept saying, "My baby is dead. My baby is dead." I didn't let go of Kathy until I saw the emergency room doctor, and gave her to him.

The doctor laid our Kathy on the examining table and put his stethoscope to her chest. In a moment he raised his head and said, "She's alive! She's in a coma from the seizures she's had, but she's still alive!" He explained that she was breathing, but so shallowly that I couldn't hear or feel her breathing. At this point my obstetrician arrived, and both Kathy and I were admitted into the hospital to recover from our ordeal.

Just a few weeks later our second child, John Michael, was born. It didn't take us long to know that I had given birth to a little maverick. All we had to do was look at the stubborn little face and we knew we were in for it. In fact, he wouldn't allow anyone to look at him when he was taking his bottle. If I glanced down at him, I would see him watching me to make sure I didn't sneak a peak at how he was doing. And if he caught me looking, he would scream and toss out the bottle. It seemed like I spent John's entire infancy staring at the ceiling.

Watching John develop over the next few months made us even more aware of the fact that Kathy was starting to decline. He slowly caught up with Kathy, and then he started passing her by. The doctor was as concerned as we were by this time. It soon became apparent that our Kathy was retarded as well as epileptic. I didn't know what to do. I didn't have anywhere to turn. Friends and family tried to help. They patted me on the shoulder, encouraged me, sometimes gushed with enthusiasm over advances they only thought they saw in Kathy. But when everybody went home and Mike was sleeping beside me, I was alone. I didn't know anybody who really understood. I ached for somebody to shield me from the pain and sorrow. I ached for somebody to assure me that Kathy really did know and understand that I loved her even the way she was and that I would never have done anything knowingly wrong that would hurt her as much as she had been hurt. I needed Jesus Christ, but I didn't even know it.

Over the years I felt a pressing need for God in my life. I have known from the earliest time I can remember that there was Someone to appeal to for help when the going got so rough that I just didn't know how I was going to make it another second. I would look up towards heaven and pray for help, but it always seemed to me that my prayers only got about as high as the ceiling. I would pray during times of stress, but I figured that unless you were one of the great men of the Bible, God wasn't likely to answer. I knew about God, but I sure didn't know him personally, or his Son, either.

The tragedy of this is that I was just like thousands of American "Christians." There are ministers in hundreds of pulpits who have never had a personal relationship with the Lord Jesus Christ. They have never preached the salvation message because they have never experienced salvation themselves. As a result, the people in their flocks don't even know about being "born again." Christianity is more than occupying a pew on Sunday. It is more than writing the word "Christian" where the form asks for one's religion. It is more than having someplace to go to show off new Easter clothes. It is having a close personal relationship with the God who created you, who loved you from the beginning of time. It is making Jesus the absolute Lord of your life. It is living daily in victory through the power of Christ living in you, saving, empowering, strengthening, and comforting.

When I look back over those next few years, I grieve over the fact that I had to go through them without the comfort and strength of the Lord. In years to come I would know the comfort of a loving Jesus whose hand I could hold when times were hard, but those first few years with Kathy found me just barely getting through with only a mother's love for her child.

CHAPTER 5

Children: A Blessing

In 1963 our daughter Laurie Michele was born. I now had three children in diapers. Mike said he never saw a woman so bent on proving the doctors wrong. Laurie was and is the image of her mother.

Laurie has been blessed with a sunny disposition. She has experienced a lot of tragedy in her life, yet she is still a happy person. As a baby she was a dream. All I had to do to keep her content for hours was to pop her into her playpen with a pile of toys and forget her. She entertained herself.

I think the good Lord was having mercy on me when he gave me Laurie. I was as busy as a one-armed paper hanger! Just keeping bottoms dry and stomachs fed kept me busy. John was a "terrible two," into everything, and Kathy was in such bad condition that she needed constant attention.

It was becoming more apparent with every passing day that Kathy was severely retarded. I had a terrible time getting food down her. I finally discovered that I could feed her in her sleep. I used to fill her bottle with a jar of baby food and milk. I'd make a huge hole in the nipple and then I would give her the bottle in her crib, while she slept. It would take so long for the whole bottle to go down that many nights Mike found me sound asleep, hanging over the crib.

Kathy's pediatrician had her under heavy medication to try to control her seizures. After a time the medication itself became a problem. Her doctor said he didn't know what else to do for her, so he sent us to a specialist in San Marino. The new doctor examined her, and after about an hour of tests he said that he thought that Kathy had a very rare kind of epilepsy. He wanted to do one more test in order to confirm his diagnosis.

Kathy was placed in front of a bank of lights at the lab. The technician turned them on and they began flashing. Almost immediately, Kathy went into a convulsion. This confirmed the doctor's suspicion. Kathy had what is called photic epilepsy. The reaction from the D.P.T. shot had damaged the optic nerve in such a way that Kathy herself could bring on seizures by focusing in on patterns. She could look at any small geometric pattern (like a polka dot dress, screening, acoustical ceilings, patterns in carpets, etc.) and bring on a seizure herself.

I asked the doctor why in the world she would deliberately bring on a seizure. His comment was that it was like a very good LSD trip. He said she liked the stimulation. I had a hard time believeing him until I read up on epilepsy and one woman made the statement that after her first seizure she would have given her life to feel that way again. Now we had to find a combination of medications that would not allow Kathy the freedom to bring on these seizures.

Her current medication was not right for her kind of seizures. First, Kathy had to be withdrawn slowly and carefully from her current medication. She was on four different drugs, and they were all habit-forming. The doctor felt she should be hospitalized to go through withdrawal. He also felt that a hospital that specialized in this type of case was best.

The next day Mike and I took our little girl to the hospital for her treatment. I will never forget that place as long as I live. There were children in every condition in that hospital: children being withdrawn from drug dependence, children with multiple handicaps, children being withdrawn from alcohol dependence, children who had been abused by their parents. The true tragedy was that a place like this had to exist at all. No wonder Jesus said, "suffer the little children to come unto me."

This hospital was used mostly for charity patients and none of the amenities I was used to from other hospitals were in evidence. There were no private rooms, only huge wards full of crying, sick, scared, and bewildered children enclosed in metal cribs. The cribs alone made me shudder. The enamel was chipped off in a million places. The surroundings were bad, but what really got to me were the sobbing children with no one to comfort them.

I didn't know what to say or do. I was in such a state of shock, seeing so much misery around me. Before I knew it, a very efficient nurse had taken Kathy from me. In just a few minutes the little girl I had brought in decked out in a ruffled pink dress, white pinafore, lace-trimmed socks, and patent leather shoes looked like all the other children. The nurse had put a ragged shirt on her and placed her in one of those ugly, peeling cribs. Briskly she told us it was time for us to leave, and she shoved us out the door.

Mike and I got in our car, looked at each other for a moment, then in unison said, "NO WAY!" We got out of the car, sneaked back into the hospital, waited for the coast to clear, grabbed our daughter, and ran.

I held Kathy so tightly all the way home that she cried. As soon as we got back to Anaheim we called the doctor and told him what we had done. The hospital had already called him with the news that she was missing. We hadn't even stopped for her clothes.

I told the doctor that we just couldn't leave her there, and asked him if we could get a private nurse and help Kathy through withdrawal at home. He told us what to do, and a week later we had her off those drugs.

With the new medication we now had better control over Kathy's seizures. We knew that she was retarded and we would have to live with that, but at least she wasn't falling on the floor with head-banging seizures anymore. We knew there wasn't much we could do for her mental condition, but she needed physical help too. She had not gained any weight in the past year, so I began to seek professional help in this area.

First I went to the doctor in San Marino who had diagnosed her epilepsy correctly, thinking he would be able also to help me with her physical health. That turned out to be a terrible mistake. When I asked him what I should do, he suggested putting her in the hospital and letting them do some tests for protein assimilation. As long as we had her in there, he thought it would be a good idea to infect her with diptheria. He said the high fever from the disease might burn out some of the scar tissue in her brain that was causing her problems. I asked him if such a drastic measure could kill her. His answer still shocks me to this day. "Well, in her physical condition that's a possibility, but you don't have much to lose, do you!"

"NOT MUCH TO LOSE! I've got a lot to lose!" I'd fought for this child's life for years and I wasn't about to take a chance on it now. I just glared at the doctor, grabbed my child, and walked out. When I got home he was on the phone to apologize for his "unthinking remark."

I told Mike what had happened, and I also told him about what I had been thinking all the way home. I said, "You know, Mike, so many people have told me to try taking Kathy to a chiropractor, and I've always thought they were crazy. Well, I've got nothing to lose after what that doctor said to me today, so I'm going to try it."

The next day I took Kathy to see Dr. David Smith. He had been highly recommended to me by several people. I told him what the specialist had recommended, and Dr. Smith almost hit the ceiling: "The man's crazy! All you have to do is look at this little thing and you know she couldn't survive something that drastic!" He said he'd work up a treatment plan and sent me home with instructions to return the next day.

We were there first thing in the morning. The minute we walked in, David handed Kathy a big glass of carrot juice. He pointed to a huge bag of carrots sitting in the corner and a vegetable juicer on the table. He told me to take these things home with a tall can of protein powder that he had ready for me, and to start feeding her any way I could.

I had always heard how chiropractors were in practice only for the money. Well, if David Smith is an example of this I'll never believe it. After the first day we were there, David would never take another cent for caring for Kathy. I tried to pay him back some for his devotion to Kathy by putting draperies from our store in his office. It was such a pleasure to have a doctor who really cared after the callous treatment we received from so many doctors before.

Kathy turned orange from all her carrots, but we didn't mind.

She gained five pounds the first month, and began a steady uphill climb. Kathy has been in perfect physical health ever since then.

Over the years, I have been approached by many parents who have to cope with the reality of retardation in their children. Some parents are able to maintain a happy, positive frame of mind, but others are totally devastated. Some parents are fiercely protective of their retarded children, but others can't begin to deal with this problem they've been handed.

I decided quite early that Kathy was mine to love and cherish. What was wrong with Kathy had to take a back seat to what was right with her. My only regret is that I didn't have a personal relationship with Jesus in those first difficult years. Things would have been so much easier.

After I came to the Lord, and grew in my relationship to him, the reality of Jesus' command, "Suffer the little children to come unto me and forbid them not, for of such is the Kingdom of Heaven," has become a beacon of light to me. Kathy will always be a child and her eternal future with Jesus is secure. Can any of us hope for a better future for our children?

CHAPTER 6

Michael, Michael

I wish I didn't have to write this chapter, because it chronicles the sad events of the end of my ten year "honeymoon." The past returned to haunt me. The previous few years had been good, even with the tragedy of Kathy.

Mike and I had been a team, working together to make a decent life for ourselves and our children. Our business was going well. Much of its success was due to my mother's help. Both Mike and I thought she was a gem. She had taken my place at the store so I could be home with the children. She was totally devoted to making the business grow, and it was growing. We didn't even have to advertise anymore. The referrals were rolling in. Every day there were more and more appointments for Mlke to go to homes, advise them on their drapery needs, and sell them custom draperies. Even contractors were calling up, and Mike bid and won contracts for several tracts of homes.

I began to get uneasy. I would think Mike was at the store but then my mother would call from there, looking for him because he had missed an appointment and his customer was annoyed. He began to miss several appointments a week, and I knew his old habits were returning. Anyone who knows Mike knows he's compulsive about being on time. He is not only punctual, he is usually early.

There was trouble at home, too. Throughout our marriage, whenever Mike was doing something he wasn't supposed to, he acted the same. If he spent too much time at the racetrack or if he had a new female liason, I could always bet and win that Mike was acting up at home. I guess he thought that if he could make it unpleasant enough, he had a good excuse not to come home.

Mike set me up this way time after time, throughout our marriage. He did it at the beginning of our marriage and he did it at the end of our marriage. I never did find a way to combat it. If I would refrain from saying anything in protest, or if I refused to fight back, he would get just that much more hateful. He would call me names, and if that didn't break me, he would start on my family. If *that* didn't work, he would start on the kids—and that's where he *always* got to me. He never said much to Laurie, but poor John got the brunt of his verbal abuse over the years. When he had me to the point of sputtering, he would complain about how miserable it was at home, and how he had to escape. I don't know, but I bet he used this same method on his first wife. He seemed too good at it to have just learned it while working on me.

As the events of each day made me more and more certain that Mike was having another affair, the knot in my stomach grew larger and larger and harder and harder. It even became difficult for me to breathe. I found out later that these are common physical manifestations of the confused emotions of a wife with an unfaithful husband. As bad as the physical symptoms were, they were not nearly as painful as my emotional turmoil was.

All wives of unfaithful husbands go through every emotion that is known to woman. First there is guilt. Women have been feeling guilt since Eve. You start searching for all the things you must have done wrong that drove your husband to cheat on you. You feel that you must have failed him in some way or he wouldn't have turned to someone else.

Sometimes you are right—there are things you could improve. You could work on your appearance, or make your conversation more interesting, or pay more attention to him. But even with your shortcomings, you still should be able to expect your husband to be faithful to you.

The next feeling you go through is anguish over the thought of being alone. Most wives work on the premise that a bad marriage is better than no marriage. Of course, this keeps the wife in bondage, because the wife is then unable to demand fidelity from her mate. This attitude is devastating to one's self-esteem. All it ever does is start a vicious pattern of self-hate that leaves you feeling like you somehow deserve the treatment you are getting.

Then you feel anger, even rage, because your husband is manipulating you into feeling all of the other negative emotions. Betrayal is a destructive force. It destroys your ability to trust and to love. It makes you frightened to make yourself vulnerable to hurt ever again.

And hurt is the emotion you feel the most. Sheer biting, gut-wrenching hurt. All you really want to do is lie down and die, just to put yourself out of your misery. No one can say anything to take away the pain, and no matter how many times you go through it, it hurts the last time just as much or even more than the first time, as long as you still love that man.

One thing I have learned over the years about affairs is that they are by their very nature self-limiting. Either the wife finds out, the husband finds out, the man gets tired of the woman, the woman gets tired of the man, or they both get tired of their mates and decide to stroll off into the sunset together. One of the above is always the conclusion. I know because I've been through each and every alternative.

The outcome this time was that the woman's husband found out. The ironic thing was that another ending was also in the works: Mike also was tired of the woman. In fact, the husband caught them together while Mike was in the middle of breaking off his relationship with her!

I knew something had happened, because the night before all of a sudden Mike was back to his own sweet self again. He was good to the children, sweet to me, and he even gave the dog a pat. This was my signal over the years that the latest woman was in the past. We all could relax until the next one came along. I'm not trying to minimize the hurt this causes, I'm just stating the facts as I had to be able to live with them.

It is also easier to cope when you don't have to come face to face with the situation. At least that way you can have a small bit of doubt with which to fool yourself. Well, unfortunately, I wasn't let off that easily this time.

My world came crashing down around me that day with a telephone call. The man on the phone stated his name, and I answered, "Oh yes, I recognize your name, you're one of our customers. We made drapes for you." He answered ,"That's not all your husband did for me! He is also having an affair with my wife!" He then told me he had found them together, and he ended by telling me that I would probably be hearing from Mike soon, because he had told Mike that he was going to call me.

I was calm after I hung up. I had that terrible knot in the pit of my stomach, but I was calm. I was calm until I saw Mike Esses walk in the door. Then I hit the ceiling. The anger I felt was so intense that I couldn't even talk at first. My anger was not only anger over this affair, but it was anger combined with anguish over all the years of working out our marriage and finally becoming a family. We were no better off than when we started. When I got my voice back, I did it all. I yelled. I screamed. I cried. Oh, how I cried, because I knew the hope that the last few years had given me was crushed and destroyed.

The evening went from bad to worse. My mother and father were at the house, trying to calm me down. Ironically, it was Mike who had called them, not me. He was trying to get them to calm me down, when the doorbell rang. Mike opened the door and there stood the husband who had called and his wife. I immediately recognized the man, who was quite prominent in our city government, and Mother recognized the wife because she was always in our store, waiting for Mike.

Mike just stood there, motionless, so I asked them in. Everyone was so *civilized*. We all sat down in the living room and I served my guests coffee. The man asked Mike what his plans were. Mike's answer was abrupt: "I'll do everything possible to get my wife to forgive me." My reply was just as abrupt: "I will never forgive him! As far as I'm concerned, she can have him on a silver platter!" Mike just mumbled, "She can't leave me...She can't leave me..." over and over.

To tell the truth, I felt sorry for the woman. She had gambled everything on Mike and he was dumping her. She started crying, saying to Mike, "You told me you loved me more than anything else in this world!" Mike coldly looked at her and replied, "I just say what I know a woman wants to hear." At that cold remark I thought her husband was going to explode.

Mother was the one who handled everything at this point. She got up and said, "I think it's time you people leave. You've got your lives to straighten out and my daughter and her husband have to deal with theirs. There is no reason to prolong this meeting. It is much too painful for everyone concerned." I don't know whether they left because of the firmness in her voice or the knowledge that it was useless to continue the conversation, but they left and I never saw them again.

When Mike and I were alone, he asked me to come into our bedroom and talk. I told him I was going to the bedroom, but I was going to go to sleep, because as far as I was concerned it was over. There was nothing to talk about.

I said, "Mike, all the time those people were here my eyes kept wandering over to the end table. Laurie's little shoes were sitting there. Mike, she's only six months old and already she can't count on her father. I know now that this family isn't getting any better deal from you than your first family did. I'm finished and I'm going to see an attorney tomorrow." There must have been a finality in my voice that Mike could hear because he didn't press me any further that night.

The next morning when I opened my eyes, Mike was sitting up in the bed looking at me. He was grinning like a Cheshire cat. The last thing in the world I expected this morning was a smiling, soon to be ex-, husband. Puzzled, I asked him what he was smiling about. Well, if I had thought of a million different reasons for why he was smiling, I would never have hit upon the answer.

Michael proceeded to tell me a story that literally left me speechless. He said he had been awakened in the middle of the night, feeling someone in the room. Standing by the bed there was a figure of a man, with a glow around him. The figure was standing with his hands stretched out toward him, and then he spoke to Mike.

Mike paused a moment, like he was gathering up the courage to continue. He said, "Then the figure spoke my name. He called me Michael and he asked me a question. He asked me, 'Why do you hate Me?' " Mike looked at me with eyes full of tears and said, "Do you know what I answered the man?" I shook my head. "I told him, 'Hate you? I don't even know who the hell you are!' "

I quietly sat waiting for what Mike was going to tell me next. "I got out of bed and wandered around the house the rest of the night. Finally I went into the den and I picked up that little Hebrew New Testament I received in the mail years ago." I knew what book he was talking about. It had been sent anonymously to Mike, but I had always thought my grandmother had sent it. She was a born-again Christian who always wanted Mike to know Jesus.

He said, "I began leafing through that Bible and I read the words of Thomas when he said he wouldn't believe the resurrection until he touched the nail prints in Jesus' hands." Mike looked at me and I could see that he was desperate for me to believe him. He continued, brokenly, "Betty Lee, I knew then that the figure standing in our bedroom was Jesus, because the hands that were stretched toward me had the nail prints in them."

Mike turned to me and said, "Betty Lee, for years now you have been trying to get me to go to church. You've said that you've known that we need to get close to God if there is any hope for our marriage. Well, after last night I couldn't agree with you more. I want to take my family to church. I want to learn about the Lord, because I know now that he is real. I gave him my life last night, and I know with his help I'll be a better man. Please honey, you've got to give our marriage another chance."

I was stunned by Mike's words. I thought, "I don't believe a word that he's said, yet what if he's telling the truth?" I had never heard of anything like this happening, but that didn't mean it couldn't happen. After all, there are a lot of things I never heard of. Finally I told him that I couldn't answer him yet, that he had to give me time to think.

Mike continued to plead with me to give him an answer, but when I wouldn't he left for the store. He finally accepted the fact that due to the bizzare turn of events, it was going to take me time to figure out what I had to do.

Mike's words, "I tell women what they like to hear," still rang in my ears. I couldn't help wondering if this was what he was doing to me. Mike knew I wanted us to go to church together. The few times I had managed to get him to church, on Easter Sunday or a Christmas Eve, I had the distinct impression that he was very uncomfortable.

This outlandish story about Jesus was just too opportune. Yet, if it were true, I would be denying a move of God to straighten out our lives. I wanted to talk to someone, but to tell the truth, I was afraid they would think I was crazy for even giving it a moment's consideration. The story was just too far out to have any validity. After all, I was from a Presbyterian background and this sort of thing just didn't happen after New Testament times.

Finally, Mike's many phone calls, the children's need for a father, the off chance that Mike's story might be true, and the dozen red roses that arrived convinced me that I had everything to gain and nothing to lose by giving it a try. I figured this time he was going to have to do something constructive. He had promised to go to church, and given some time, I would know whether his story was true. After all, a born-again experience is supposed to change your life. My thought was, "We'll see."

CHAPTER 7

God's Transforming Power

The words of the doxology rang down from the high vaulted ceiling of the First Presbyterian Church of Anaheim. Mike, the children, and I sat in the first pew. This was a very special day. In just a few minutes our new little son, Donald Gard Esses, was going to be baptized and dedicated to the Lord. Dr. Donald Gard, our Pastor and our friend, and our baby's namesake, would officiate at the ceremony.

This was one of those rare days when everything went right, when I could exclaim honestly, "It is well with my soul." My spirit was soaring with the music, my children were behaving like little angels, I was proud of my husband, my dearest friends were gathered around us, and miracle of miracles, my hair turned out great.

The sleeping baby, who lay so peacefully in my arms, was the perfect result of the last couple of years. Life had become sweet again, and this church and its people had helped make it that way.

I don't know what I had expected when we started to attend the Presbyterian church, but I had never expected it to be as rewarding as it was. We had made such good friends there. Glenn and Alyson Fry were now our dearest friends, and would be a source of solace and comfort to me in all the coming years.

Don Gard and his wife Ruth were also very special to us. Mike admired Don, and Don in turn took Mike under his wing. When we found that I was pregnant again, Mike prayed for a boy, because he wanted to name him after his pastor. It was a wonderful day when Donnie was born, because I was able to give Mike the desire of his heart. Little did we know on the day of Donnie's dedication, when we gave him to God, how soon the Lord was going to take us up on our offer.

Our troubles seemed to be all in the past as we immersed ourselves more and more into the activities of the church. Mike began teaching a class on the Old Testament, and we both got involved with the Mariners, the social and service arm of the Presbyterian Church. This is where we made all our friends.

Within the next couple of years we held many positions in the church. Mike was a deacon, then he became an elder. We were the leaders (Admirals) of the Mariners. Mike held the position of head of stewardship, and then when Dr. Gard left to take a church back east, Michael became part of the pastoral search committee.

In retrospect, I know Mike was allowed to advance much too rapidly into the leadership of the church. There was no way that he, as a new Christian, could have grown spiritually mature enough to handle properly the positions he coveted and then won. All his accomplishments served to do was to make him feel important and to think he didn't need anything or anyone. And yet, it wasn't all the fault of the church, either. Mike was eager and willing to do anything that needed to be done there. He volunteered for everything and spent so much time there that he seemed like a permanent fixture. The church was never overflowing with such eager and dedicated volunteers, so it's no wonder that they took advantage of Mike and used him as much as they did. The problem stemmed from his immaturity in Christ and his long-seated inability to cope with power and prestige. Everybody thought Mike was great, and Mike thought so too. Unfortunately, this made him very vulnerable to corruption.

Don Gard's leaving the church was a terrible blow to Mike. He dearly loved this man. In fact, even though they were about the same age, he gave Don the love and respect of a son for a father. (I watched Mike do exactly the same thing a few years later with Ralph Wilkerson.) Mike was grieved with Don's leaving the church, and I think to a certain extent he felt like a child who had been abandoned.

After Don left, Earl Mason, who had been the assistant pastor, became interim pastor. A short time later Dr. Ralph Didier was selected to become our senior pastor. Then Mike became head elder of the church, which at that time had a membership of about 2,500. In 1968 Mike was elected president of the church. He also was nominated vice president of the United Presbyterian Synod of southern California.

Everyone was thrilled with Mike's progress. My mother and father, Mike's brother and his wife, and our close friends, who knew how bad things had been, were convinced he had changed for good. The men in the church thought he was the best thing that had happened to the church in a long time, not only because of his ability to teach and administrate, but because of the rapid spiritual progress he appeared to be making. Dr. Didier even took me out to lunch one day to talk to me about Mike becoming his assistant instead of bringing in another pastor. Dr. Didier thought he would be a tremendous help to him because Mike seemed to have his finger on the pulse of the church.

There was only one person who was not happy with Michael's progress, and that was me. I lived with him, and I saw the real Michael Esses at home. The man who for the past couple of years had been a devoted husband and loving father was rapidly disappearing. The danger signals were starting again. The familiar cockiness, the filthy language, and once more the old, so familiar absences from home. Only this time it was different. This time I felt caught in a trap.

We were no more just the owners of a local drapery shop. Now, Michael was president of a church. Now, eyes were on our Christian walk. Now, I found it impossible to go to my pastor for counsel, because as far as he was concerned Mike was his right-hand man. Michael was known as a man of God. In fact, he was such a man of God that Jesus himself had appeared to him in order to bring him into the fold. He was a Jew who had accepted his Messiah. Now, how do I tell anyone I suspect he is involved in another affair?

I didn't know where to go for help. I knew I couldn't go to any man, and I really didn't know Jesus well enough to go to him. My girlfriend Alyson had been telling me about a local church she had been visiting once in a while. She said it was quite different from what we were used to, but she said you could feel the Spirit of God there. I thought maybe if I went there I could get some direction.

Nothing Alyson said prepared me for the following Thursday morning at the Christian Center prayer meeting. I sat quietly in the back row thinking, "I'll just observe and see if I can see or even maybe feel what Alyson is talking about." It didn't take me long to realize that I had never seen anything like this before. I heard people praying for themselves, for others, for their wants, and for their needs. They prayed with power and conviction and so much faith, that they were already thanking the Lord at the end of their prayers that the answers to those prayers were already an accomplished fact.

Most of the songs weren't in the song books. They were straight from the Bible. I had never sung songs like this before, and I said a silent thanks to Alyson for telling me to bring my Bible. It was amazing how much more joy and praise was expressed when God's own words were sung back to him.

I realized that these people had something I didn't have. At the end of the meeting, when Paston Wilkerson stood and gave the message of salvation, I realized what was missing. I had never been born-again! These people knew Jesus, and I only knew about him. The desire for a personal relationship with the Lord had always been with me, but I had never been shown how to get it, how to be saved.

Mine wasn't the only denominational church to fail its people concerning salvation. So many churches assume that if you are in their churches, you are automatically a Christian. They teach you how to lead an ethical life. They teach you how to live with your fellow man. They base their sermons on scripture, and tell you how to apply the Word of God to your life. All these things are good and solid, and I must admit that I met the most honest, ethical, and inherently decent people I know in that Presbyterian Church.

I had been raised with all the fundamental values of my home church. My folks were honest, decent, and ethical. Where a very basic problem occurs is that many good but unsaved people come in contact with people who call themselves born-again Christians, and yet these "Christians" don't walk their talk. Their honesty is more than questionable and their decency leaves much to be desired. How are you going to tell people who are basically good that they need what these people have? My folks, for example, watched Michael in action for years, and believe me, they didn't want what he had.

Calling ourselves born-again and spirit-filled Christians is a great responsibility. The leaders of the denominational churches are not stupid men. If they could see the evidence of wholeness, responsibility, dedication to God, ethical behavior, basic decency, and humility in the lives of "Born-againers," they would seek and teach salvation.

Mike was getting meaner by the day at home. If you saw him in public, you would have thought him the happiest man alive, but at home his language was getting more and more abusive. I used to think I'd have to record him swearing for anyone to believe me.

I was going to bed alone night after night, not knowing where he was or when he would be home. The usual feeble excuses were offered. Suddenly there were dozens of out of town customers who could only see him at night. Sometimes his story was that the customers took so long to make their decisions, it was just too late to drive the 30 or 40 miles back home. Sometimes it was that the weather was too bad to return home until morning.

I continued going over to Christian Center every chance I got, mostly on Sunday nights and Thursday mornings. I was so filled with longing to experience the joy I could see on all those faces, that I couldn't stay away if I tried. It wasn't at Christian Center, though, that I met the Lord. It was at my friend Alyson's home. I had gone over to Alyson's house to talk to her. She knew I was unhappy and that I was going through some problems in my marriage. I didn't tell Alyson what the problem was because her husband, Glenn, and Mike were both elders at the church.

I talked about the relationship with Jesus I could see the people at Christian Center had, and I said that I longed for such a relationship. It didn't take Alyson a second to get down on her knees by the coffee table and tell me to join her. She said, "Betty, if you want to know Jesus, he is here right this moment to answer your call."

Alyson began to pray for me and before I knew it, I broke into a million pieces. A flood of tears started flowing that I thought would never stop, and a flow of happiness began that I prayed would never cease. That was how I met Jesus. It wasn't very dramatic, but it was real, and he has never left me since that day, and I know he never will.

That night I sat down with a copy of John Sherrill's *They Speak With Other Tongues*, and began to read. At one point the author said to stop reading and ask Jesus for the Baptism of the Holy Spirit, right at that moment. I knew from the teaching I had received at Christian Center that this baptism was a gift to God's people and I was entitled to it.

I had heard people sing and pray in the spirit at Christian Center, and it touched me so much that my knees would get weak and I could hardly stand. I was so thrilled with my new relationship with the Lord that I wanted all God had to give me. Once more I dropped to my knees. I buried my head in the pillow on the chair, and started praying. It seemed no time at all before my words began to change from English to a heavenly language. The angels had nothing on me at that moment—I was in paradise.

It tells us in the Bible that Jesus is always on time. Well, his timing was perfect for me. A few days after I met the Lord I needed to cling to him as never before, and he was there for me. Even though I was having a terrible time with Mike in our marriage, I was still totally unprepared to come home one day and find that he had packed everything that belonged to him and had vanished into thin air. Alyson called and said Mike had called her. He told her that I was going to need her, and added that I was never going to see him again.

How do I tell of the turmoil of the next few days? It was hard for me to imagine anyone, even Mike, leaving a family under such trying circumstances. Glenn and Alyson came over and Dr. Didier, did, too. They were all trying to help me figure out what to do.

I had four little kids to take care of, and I had to run the store, because that was going to have to be my livelihood. My mother was in the hospital, seriously ill after major surgery. I couldn't even tell her what had happened, much less depend on her to help me with the business. So, my first priority was a baby sitter. I put an ad for a housekeeper in the paper, lined up some neighborhood girls to take care of the older children when they got out of school, took Donnie and his toys under my arm, and headed for the store.

Financially I was in terrible shape. Mike had emptied the savings account, and our joint checking account was overdrawn by $2,000. Glenn quickly went to the bank and covered the checks for me. A couple of days later, he came to my rescue again. I came out of the house to take the children to school and to go to work and found my car gone. It had been repossessed because Mike had not made the payment on it. Glenn went to the car pound and paid what was needed to get it released.

The first few days after Mike left were filled with trying to stabilize things. The horrendous mess had one side benefit. I didn't have much time to brood over Mike, only over the mess he had left. I was coasting on the energy from a great deal of anger. I couldn't imagine any man being this cruel to his family.

It was hard at home with my children. I hadn't figured out a way to tell them that they would probably never see their father again. I knew Mike had never seen his other family again, even though they only lived a few miles away. Finally I just took the doorknob off of his closet door, so they couldn't blunder in and find all of his clothes gone. Then I told the kids that their father had gone to visit his brother. I just wasn't ready to deal with their trauma as yet, not when I was unable to cope with my own.

Well, now it was out in public. I didn't have to hide what was happening at home anymore. I knew that Dr. Didier was terribly disappointed in Mike. I decided that I didn't want to tell him all the rest of the garbage. After all, Mike was the president of his church. Finally I went to see Pastor Wilkerson at Christian Center.

I told Pastor that I knew Mike had left with another woman, and I filled him in on Mike's background. I told him about Mike's abandonment of his first family and now of us. After I finished talking, Pastor looked at me and said, "Betty, you better start 'Praising the Lord.' "

I looked at the man like he was crazy. I asked him, "What in

God's name do I have to praise him about?" Pastor just looked at me and said, "What else can you do?" I thought about it for a minute, and recalled the teaching I had received at this church, and I began to see the simple logic in Pastor's words.

I thought, "Jesus knows everything that's going to happen to me. So he has prepared me to go through this battle. He has become my Lord and my Savior. He has given me the gift of his Holy Spirit. Now he is telling me, 'I will see you through this valley, if you will hold tight to my hand. All this will do to you is build your faith, if you cling to me.'"

I had been taught at Christian Center to give my burden to the Lord. He had said in his word that the battle is not ours, it is the Lord's. That meant that I didn't have to deal with Mike. The Lord would, and in the meantime he would take care of my family and my finances if I would do my part. I had already learned the lesson that God does for us what we can't do, and he expects us to do what we can do. I knew without a shadow of a doubt that if I worked as hard as I could for my family, Jesus would give me success.

I know that sometimes money is about the most difficult area in which to trust God, but the excellent teaching and the example of Pastor Wilkerson had already taught me this lesson. Pastor would say from the pulpit, "The day I have to ask for money is the day I leave the ministry. The Lord knows our needs, and he will tell the people what to give, I don't have to say a word." Pastor put his teaching into practice. All he ever said about money at that time was, "It is now time for your tithes and offerings."

I tried very hard to follow Pastor's advice. Every time I thought about Mike I said, "Praise the Lord." In years to come I would get a chance to teach on this subject. At first I really didn't mean "Praise the Lord," and I was aware Jesus knew I didn't mean it, but I would tell him that I was going to keep on saying it until he helped me mean it.

I was really too busy during the day to give my situation much thought. All I could think about was juggling baby sitters around so I could make my sales calls in the evenings. I wasn't able to make any of these appointments during the day, because I was tied to the store and little Donnie. When I finally fell into bed at night, I was too tired even to dream.

Daily I kept saying "Praise the Lord" and gradually I realized that I was beginning to mean it. The anger was gone completely. Now I was hurting, but even that was starting to subside. I still cried myself to sleep most nights, but this time Mike's leaving didn't hold the terror that it always had before. There was a difference this time, and the difference was Jesus.

One thing I couldn't help wondering about was why Jesus hadn't made any difference in Mike's life. Why was he still the same? After I met the Lord I changed, I began growing. I was reacting differently in this situation because I was not the same. Yet, I had not seen such a change in Mike. Yes, the first couple of years after the Lord appeared before him, Mike behaved himself, but this was the same as he had done before when he was caught in an affair. The same old pattern was there. He was like a person with a chronic disease that goes into periodic remission. The symptoms leave, but the disease is still there.

I thought after you have a born-again experience, something more than remission happens. I know you are at the same point in your life before and after this experience. Yet, at that point, you change the direction in which your life is going. Instead of walking toward hell, you turn and start walking toward heaven. I thought, "There has to be some growth, even if it's slight." But, here was Mike, doing exactly the same thing he had done before he met the Lord. Because of the children involved it was more irresponsible.

A possible answer to this puzzle was given to me by Earl Mason, who was the assistant pastor at the Presbyterian Church. He told me Mike had confided that he had made up the story about Jesus appearing to him in order to stop me from divorcing him. That made sense. I didn't like it, but it made sense.

At dawn one morning, the phone rang. I knew who it was before I answered. It was Mike calling from Miami, asking if he could come home. I know he expected me to be totally hysterical, but that was not the case. I had already made peace with the situation, so there was no need to get excited. I just told him this was his home and he would always be welcome in it.

Mike's homecoming, a few days later, was not what he expected. He arrived at suppertime. When he walked in, John and

Laurie were sprawled on the floor in front of the television, watching cartoons. They barely glanced up to say, "Hi Daddy." After all, he had only been away on a visit, as far as they were concerned. I was in the kitchen making supper, while Kathy and Donnie were busy with their coloring books at the table.

Donnie squealed when he saw his daddy, and I kissed him hello, but that was how we usually greeted him when he got home from work. I knew from the look on Mike's face that he had expected either a brass band and banners, saying "Welcome home," or to be castigated by each and every one of us. What he hadn't expected was the matter-of-fact way we accepted him back into our lives.

Ever since Mike's phone call asking to come home, I had been doing a lot of thinking. I had finally decided not to say anything about what Earl had told me. I knew Mike would just deny it, so I was better off keeping silent. I figured if he doesn't know that I know, he will have to continue to go to church. I thought at least in church he would be exposed to the Lord. I paid dearly for this decision, because in the years to come, I would hear Mike testify about Jesus appearing to him over and over again, while I had to remain silent.

Dr. Didier had tried to spare his congregation from finding out about Michael's disappearance. He bent over backward trying to be kind to him, but enough people knew that it was uncomfortable for Mike. He knew there were some who would never trust him fully again.

Mike and I decided the best thing for our marriage and family was to join Christian Center, where no one knew Mike yet. I insisted that Mike meet with Pastor Wilkerson first, so he would be able to help Mike with his problems. Pastor Wilkerson accepted Mike with open arms, told him he was sure Mike's problems were now over, and asked him to teach at Christian Center just as he had at the Presbyterian church.

I was surprised that Pastor let Mike teach when Mike had just come back from an affair, had been married before, and had abandoned another family. I had thought fundamental churches frowned on those things. I figured I must have been wrong.

I have to confess one thing that happened shortly after Mike's return. My own actions showed me I wasn't as mature in the Lord as I had at first thought. We were sitting at the table eating supper. Donnie was being a typical three year old. He was fussing about his food. He was whining and complaining and being a nuisance. I've never to this day, figured out why Mike did what he did, but before I knew it, he had picked up Donnie's bowl of spaghetti and dumped it over his head. Donnie wasn't whining anymore: he was screaming.

I looked at that scene and was horrified. I realized later that I was reacting to more than just the bowl of spaghetti. I was reacting also to the hurt and anger of the weeks that lay behind me. All I knew then was that "Mama Bear" went into action, and I punched Mike in the mouth so hard that I broke all the caps on his front teeth.

That was so unlike me. I had never hit anyone in my life before. The closest I had ever come to hitting was the few spankings I had given my kids. Hitting was just not in my nature. Yet, I had just punched Mike out. Mike told me later that from the look on my face, if I had had a gun in my hand, he would have been dead. Later I used this incident many times to point out a truth: The only thing you truly have control of, is what you give God to control. When you try to control anything yourself, it is always subject to your losing control.

CHAPTER 8

Taken By Fire

There came a time when, as much as I wanted to, I couldn't protect my Donnie. As a parent the guilt will always be with me. When a woman gives birth the overwhelming need to protect her child is also born, and it never goes away.

It was a few days before Christmas. Our lives had settled down to routine once again. The trauma of Mike's departure and return was now a thing of the past, and we were looking forward to the holiday season. Michael was at the dining room table preparing his Bible lesson for the following week. The girls and I were lying on my bed watching the Christmas shows on T.V. John and Donnie were running around playing, in my room one moment, then gone the next.

Suddenly I heard Mike yell, "FIRE!" I jumped up and ran towards the living room, spotting John along the way. I yelled at him, *"GET A HOSE! GET A HOSE!"* and we ran out the front door together to get the hose. By the time we got the water turned on, we couldn't get back in, because the fire had started in the front room, and that was already engulfed. The windows were already being blown out.

Black smoke was billowing out the front door, and the house was plunged into darkness. I could hear Mike getting the children out the back door, so all I could think to do was try to comfort the one I had with me. I put my arms around John and we stood there, trying to comprehend what was going on. John and I started around the house and met Mike and the girls coming the other way.

I took one look at them and started shouting, *"DONNIE! WHERE'S DONNIE?"* One look at Mike's face told me the answer. He hadn't gotten Donnie out. He had thought Donnie was with me. Both of us were hit with total terror when the realization that Donnie was still in that inferno hit us. I was told later that it took three men to hold me from going back into that house.

By this time, the house was totally engulfed in flames. The firemen were battling desperately to get into the house, because they knew there was a small child somewhere in that holocaust. Fireman after fireman tried to enter the house, only to be driven back by the force of the flames. It became clear, even to me, that there was no way that Donnie could still be alive.

The last few moments of Donnie's young life, I would have given the rest of my life to change. They will haunt me till the day I die. I know my child must have been so frightened, so alone, so scared, crying for his mother to rescue him. After all, hadn't I always been there for him? He was my baby, and I was supposed to protect him. All the logic in the world will not release me from this pain. I will carry it with me until I can hold him in my arms once more, and tell him how sorry I am.

I know the truth to a parable I often have heard: God sometimes takes the baby lambs to be with him, because he knows the sheep will surely follow. I will always follow Jesus, because I know Donnie is with him. I also know that as much as I love that baby, Jesus loves him more. When you have lost a child, you realize just exactly what the Father sacrificed when he put his son on the cross.

The knowledge that Donnie was with Jesus was the only thing that saved my sanity. I look at people who don't believe and I wonder how in the world they get through something this hard. How could they exist, or why would they bother, if this world was all that there is? I know that it was the knowledge that I was going to see Donnie again that brought me through this agony intact.

To the many people who want the magic word to cushion their shock at a time like this, there is only one word I can give you that will help you through the despair, the hurt, and the anguish you will feel. That word is Jesus. You will notice I didn't say he will keep you from feeling these pains, but he will help you bear them.

Many Christians I have talked with are being bombarded on both sides: from one side by whatever grief they are going through, and from the other side by the guilt they feel because they are feeling such grief.

We are all human beings with human vulnerabilities, and when we experience the beautiful emotion of love, there is a price we pay. God made us this way. God himself is this way. If he didn't grieve over the treatment of his son, Jesus would not have been the marvelous sacrifice for us that he was.

Yet many well-meaning Christians feel they are failing when they feel grief. This is not their failure. If there is a failure, it is wanting to be without feeling. Love is like everything else that is wonderful, good, and precious. It is bought with a price.

The children's response to Donnie's death shows the triumph of believing in Jesus. I was the one who told my children about Donnie. Roy and Shirley Erickson, our next-door neighbors, had taken the children into their home as soon as they realized what was happening. This was especially touching because they were still in pain themselves from the death a few months before of their son Mark from leukemia.

Mike couldn't face the children, so my father went with me to the bedroom where my children were waiting. Their reaction to the news of their brother's death was beautiful, and quite a witness to my father. I had expected tears but what I got was jealousy! Both John and Laurie were quite put out with the Lord for taking Donnie instead of them. They even reminded me that the Lord already had Donnie's playmate, Mark, waiting in heaven for him. I think they smelled a set-up, with Jesus playing favorites!

By this time all of our friends were at the house. Pastor Wilkerson was there, and Glenn and Alyson Fry. Gene and Jody Brewer arrived and Jody took the shoes off her feet, and put them on mine. The children's pediatrician, Dr. Robert Curtis, came and then left in search of an all-night drug store so he could get Kathy's anti-convulsant medicine as quickly as possible.

Finally the fire was out, and the firemen were able to sift through the rubble for Donnie's body. They finally found him in the den huddled behind what was left of the couch, where he had been hiding. The autopsy later revealed that he had died of smoke inhalation, before the flames got to him.

Glenn and Alyson had us bring the family to their house until we could think clearly enough to make plans. Mike and I went to bed that night, two people in the same bed, but each in separate worlds. I don't know what Mike was thinking, but I was starting to put together my own private little hell.

It wasn't that I wasn't sure of where Donnie was now; my problem was that I couldn't come to terms with where and how he was found. You see, before I heard Mike yell, *"FIRE!"* I heard him yell at the boys. I remembered meeting John in the hall, on my way out to the living room, and he was already crying. So I lay in bed that night and began to put two and two together, and I came up with the knowledge that Donnie was hiding behind the couch from the wrath of his father. That couch had always been his hiding place when he was in trouble. A shudder went through me when I thought, "Oh God, is that why they weren't able to get him out?"

Frantically, I tried to reason with myself. I thought my imagination was going wild because of the shock of what happened. I thought I was having the normal human weakness of wanting something or someone to blame for what had happened. We don't want to believe that sometimes we have no control over what happens in our lives.

Finally I was able to shove all of these thoughts far enough to the back of my mind that I was able to forget them for awhile. I started praying for the oblivion of sleep, and the next thing I knew it was morning.

A few days later the funeral was held and Pastor Wilkerson officiated. The chapel was packed with people from the Christian Center, the Presbyterian church, and many of our friends we had made in the business world.

It was a beautiful service. When Pastor asked me what I wanted, I said, "Pastor, make it a message of salvation, because my salvation is the only reason they are not burying me with my child. I want everyone who comes to hear this message. I grieve, but as the scripture says, not like one with no hope."

How do you put your life together again, after a tragedy like this? First and foremost, a member of your family is lost, but the additional trauma is that everything else is lost, too. We ran out of the house that night with nothing but the clothing on our backs. Everything else we owned went up in smoke. There was virtually nothing left of the accumulation of a lifetime of living. House, furniture, clothing, snapshots, momentos, everything, gone.

One of our neighbors who was in the real estate business came to us and said that we were welcome to use one of his houses until our home was rebuilt. Another friend of mine, Jean Marshall, said she would co-ordinate things for us while we were at Glenn and Alyson's.

A few days later, when we walked into our temporary home, it was evident just how much Jean had accomplished. We could hardly believe our eyes when we looked around us. The house was complete. It was as if a family had been living there for years. Apparently, contributions had been pouring in ever since the fire. Every room was completely furnished. There were televisions, beds, chests, chairs, rugs, lamps, and pictures on the walls. A lovely sectional couch graced the living room. This room also announced that it was still Christmas, with a beautifully decorated Christmas tree, piled high with presents for the children. We learned that the tree and gifts were donated to us by a nearby chain drugstore.

In the kitchen was every appliance known to man, and a few that I had never seen before. Every cupboard was stocked to overflowing with canned goods. The garage was piled high with cases of more canned goods that just wouldn't fit inside.

The closets were jammed with clothes for all of us. These had been supplied by people and department stores. There were bed linens, towels, blankets, pillows, and a washer and dryer to clean all these things when they got dirty. Even the refrigerator was filled with butter, eggs, milk, and casseroles cooked by the wonderful, caring women of our community. Everything was complete, down to the salt and pepper shakers sitting on the stove.

The stream of goods continued to pour in, even after we began living in the house. I never knew when I answered the doorbell whether it would be the mailman or a turkey, an old friend or a new one with a cake in her hands. Finally, I went to Pastor Wilkerson and asked him to tell the people we had all we could possibly need or use. He told me not to discourage people from giving. He said, "They need to give, more than you need to receive." So, I contacted an agency in town that helped people who were in need, and began funneling these extra gifts over to them.

I was very grateful to all the people who helped us during these trying days, but it also gave me a problem. We were more than adequately insured and even had a policy which paid our expenses until we were back in our own home. In a very short time it became apparent that financially we were going to make a big profit from the fire. Thousands and thousands of dollars were sent to us during this time, and I begged Mike to give it to the church, to charity, or to any other relief agency. I just couldn't come to terms with making money because of Donnie's death.I knew the front page picture of my beautiful little boy had stirred people's hearts since most of these contributions were from total strangers. I spent days writing letters of appreciation for the overwhelming outpouring of help. My problem was, every time I would see Mike opening one of those envelopes and counting that money, I would go dead inside. I was never able to make him understand how I felt.

I knew that if we had used the money to help others, then I could have looked upon it as a memorial to my baby, and I would have been able to appreciate the kindness of God's people. As it was I think this contributed to the animosity I began to feel toward Mike in the subsequent weeks.

Another incident related to the fire seemed to confirm my doubts about Mike's sincerity. He had reported to the insurance company that when he sat down on the night of the fire to prepare his lesson at the dining room table, he had removed two diamond rings and his watch and laid them on the table. After the fire, they could never be found, so the insurance company paid Mike their replacement value.

A couple of months later I found the rings and watch hidden at our business. I had decided to clean out our file cabinet, and there they were, wrapped carefully in tissue. I confronted Mike and begged him to tell the insurance company they had been found, Michael refused. He told me to keep my mouth shut and he put the rings and watch into his safety deposit box.

I felt like I was being boxed in again, but I didn't know what I could do about it. So many people had their eyes on our Christian walk at this time, that I was unable to say or do anything to discourage them. I went to Pastor Wilkerson with my problem, but all he encouraged me to do was submit to Mike and let the Lord work things out.

I now had such mixed emotions toward the Lord that I could hardly deal with them. I was so grateful to him, because I had the security of knowing Donnie was safe with him, but I felt that I had to pay the price for that security by covering for Mike so God's people wouldn't be hurt. I'm not saying these were God's terms, I'm saying these are the terms I copied from others around me and set up for myself

I was a new Christian, and I was in the limelight of the Christian world, long before teaching and growth in the Lord taught me what he expects and what he doesn't expect. I have seen this happen over and over again to new Christians. If they could be used or they were well known, too often, well before they were mature in the Lord, they were given center stage and it destroyed them.

I learned this fairly early, through some of the many mistakes I made and that's why I sat under the teaching of two mature Christians, Rob and Grace Robley, for years. I've never known two people who walk closer to the Lord. It was not that I never saw them make a mistake, it was that they always remained teachable, and they taught the people under their wings to stay teachable, too.

My feelings against Mike seemed to grow every day. One evening, after another disagreement which left me on the floor being kicked by this man, I ran out of the house and headed for the cemetery. I still remember vividly lying on Donnie's grave, crying out to God my anger at him for bringing Mike back into my life and taking my son from me instead. I found myself yelling, *"GIVE HIM BACK TO ME! GIVE HIM BACK TO ME!"*

I had finally spoken out what was in my heart, and this was the catharsis I needed in order to deal with the turmoil that was inside. I finally admitted to myself that I blamed Mike for Donnie's death, and that I was mad at God for allowing this to happen. I knew that every time since the fire that Mike had disappointed me with his behavior I was saying to God, "See who you brought back to me, and look at what you took from me instead!" I told the Lord, "I don't know how I'll ever forgive you."

Years later I taught on this subject. Most of us know that we have to forgive our enemies. We have to forgive our loved ones and our friends, but most of us won't admit that who we are really mad at is God. We don't like what he has allowed in our lives, and we have a hard time forgiving him for it. We fail to see our own responsibility for what happens to us, and the lessons God wants us to learn from our mistakes are often lost on us.

It was Alyson who finally managed to set me straight. I went to her and said; "Al, I'm mad at God!" I said that if Mike hadn't been there to yell at Donnie the night of the fire, I would still have my boy. I kept saying, "I wish Mike was back in Miami with his girlfriend, and my son was here with me."

Alyson, bless her, ministered to me with understanding and wisdom. She didn't make me feel like a terrible person for having such thoughts, but she did point out some truths to me.

She said, "In the first place, Betty, you prayed to God that he would bring Mike back home, and he answered your prayer. In the second place, Mike's yelling at the boys was a natural reaction at the time, because they were playing around the tree where the fire started. Third, did it ever occur to you that if Mike hadn't been here, to carry your girls out of the house, you might have lost them, too? Betty, you have to accept the fact that it was Donnie's time to go home. God made this decision, no one else. You heard those words at the funeral, 'The Lord gives, and Lord takes away: blessed be the name of the Lord.' " After my talk with Alyson, I was much more open to the Lord, and he ministered to me just a few days later.

I was awakened early on a Sunday morning totally devastated by a dream. In the dream, Donnie was alive and well, playing with his brother and sisters. This was the first time I had dreamed about him since the funeral.

I tiptoed in and checked the children in their beds, and grief washed over me even more because Donnie was not snuggled down with them. I felt my heart break in two as I stood and looked down on my sleeping children.

I dropped to my knees, put my head on one child's bed and began to pour out my sorrow to God. I found myself praying, "Oh Jesus, if you are real and Donnie is with you, please show me somehow. My heart is breaking over my baby, and my grief is causing me to have doubts that I don't want to have."

Finally, I left the children's room and went to the kitchen to put some coffee on. The silence of the house seemed to intensify my grief, so I reached over and turned on the television. I wanted some sound in the room to occupy my mind. When the picture came into focus, it was of a country scene, and the words, 'Let Us Pray,' were printed over the picture. The minister's voice began to pray and all the words I needed to hear began to pour over me.

The words told me to stand still and know that God cared and was aware of our troubles and our sorrows. The minister prayed that Jesus would comfort the bereaved, the widowed, the hurting. He prayed thanks that the Lord was our solace, our rock, our salvation. The prayer contained all the words that I needed to soothe me and give me relief from my grief and my doubts.

I was already rejoicing when the announcer's voice came over the air saying, "The meditation this morning was given by Dr. Donald Gard of the First Presbyterian Church in Anaheim." I started to cry then because God had given me the godfather of my child to pray for me. Later I called Don, who was then Professor of Religion at Fullerton College, and asked him about his prayer. He told me that it had been taped three or four years before for the television station.

I don't think it was coincidence that the studio technician pulled that particular tape to play that morning. It aired only five minutes after I had prayed, "Please show me somehow that you are real and my son is with you." As much of a miracle as the healing words of the prayer were, it was even more of a miracle that they had been prepared for me years in advance. The scripture in Isaiah 65:24 became real to me that day: "And it shall be that before they call I will answer, and while they are yet speaking I will hear."

CHAPTER 9

Familiar Patterns

The next few months passed in a whirlwind of activity. I had no idea the rebuilding of our home would be such a tremendous undertaking. I went around with a tape measure in one hand and a calculator in the other. I was measuring and planning, selecting and buying, pouring over House Beautiful and driving the contractor crazy. I would go to the house and present him with a swatch of just the right color of frosted delicate pink, with the barest hint of violet, and hear him yell to the painter, "PAINT IT PINK!" The man had no heart.

It was a wonderful day when we moved back into our home. There had never been a question in my mind about going back to the place of the fire. Many people thought we should sell and buy someplace else, but for me, being there was a comfort.

Mike was kept busy between our business and Christian Center. Pastor Wilkerson put him in charge of the men's retreat. He had run several retreats for the Presbyterian Church, so he had the experience. This is how we first met Bob and Marie DeBlase. Bob worked with Mike on the retreat and it didn't take long before Bob and Marie became our very good friends.

I began to study the scriptures in earnest at this time. I would steep myself in the lessons of Rob and Grace Robley. You could sum up their teaching in these words: practical Christian living. They taught how to live your life with the help and guidance of Jesus, day by day. The food they gave me will nourish me the rest of my life.

I think this was a lot of Mike's problem. He was never taught. After he started attending church, he was always put to work teaching, when he should have been taught himself. Just because he knew the Old Testament and could read Hebrew didn't mean he had any idea what it was like to live a committed Christian Life.

I listened to him counsel a woman over the phone one day, and realized how ignorant he was of some of the basic principles of Christianity. The woman had a husband with a roving eye, and she wanted to know how to handle the problem. Mike told her to send flowers to herself, so her husband would think she had someone else who was interested in her!

Mike's problem was that all of his knowledge was head knowledge. It apparently never made the trip to his heart. Mike later wrote the book, *The Phenomenon of Obedience*, without ever having practiced obedience himself. He knew the consequences of disobedience. After all, the Old Testament as well as the New Testament warns about that. But as Mike once remarked to me, "Rules are made for others, not for me."

I went to Grace and Rob several times and asked them to help me deal with Mike, especially after it became clear that there was another woman in the picture again. Michael, of course, denied it, so they were able to work only with me. They taught me to lean on the Lord and not lose my faith because of Mike's behavior. The first thing they made clear to me was that I couldn't blame any of this on God. Mike was my choice for a husband, not God's. I began to realize that the problems I had with Mike were making me grow more in the Lord. The Robleys taught me well that you grow more in the valleys, where the fertilizer abounds, than on the mountain tops.

The woman Mike was involved with was married and had two children. Mike would bring both husband and wife to our house for social evenings, and it was obvious that he was interested in the wife. Every time I turned around they were off in a corner together. Her husband was even starting to notice something was wrong, but he, like me, couldn't prove it. Mike was teaching a Bible study in this couple's home in a nearby town. If I dared to object and say anything about the relationship, I was told I was a tool of Satan, trying to stop Mike from teaching for God.

Sometimes it seems the attack of Satan is never so strong as when you need an abundance of faith. Mike couldn't have been more frustrating, and it was difficult for me to prepare enthusiastically for the arrival at Christian Center of the great woman of faith, Kathryn Kuhlman. I had been watching Miss Kuhlman on television, and I marveled at how powerfully Jesus used this woman. I can't tell you how excited I was when I heard she was coming to Christian Center, for our annual summer Charismatic Clinic. I couldn't help wondering if this visit wouldn't help Kathy. Everyone else in need of healing was probably wondering the same thing.

As the day of her arrival drew closer, my faith seemed to grow by leaps and bounds. I told everyone that I was going to take Kathy. I even told my mother and father, who really didn't understand about miracle healing. They still encouraged me to take their little granddaughter. I told Glenn and Alyson and Earl and Harriet. They were going to be in Ensenada, but said they would be in prayer for Kathy all the time we were gone.

The only one who tried to discourage me was Mike. I will never forget bundling my little girl into the car while I listened to filthy language flow out of her father's mouth. Kathryn Kuhlman was called every four letter word known to man, and I was called all those words, too, for taking Kathy to see her.

When I arrived at the church that next morning, there were cars parked for blocks around. Finally I found a place about six blocks away, and I parked and started walking Kathy to the church. I can't begin to tell you how I felt. I was so alone. I needed my child's father with me to want this as much as I did, but I had left him behind swearing at me.

It would have been much easier if my friends were there. I knew how much they all wanted Kathy's healing. I wished they weren't miles away, out of the country. Kathy was stumbling along, her co-ordination so bad that she kept falling. She needed to be carried, but she was too heavy for me. As I continued supporting my child as best I could, the loneliness began to engulf me.

Suddenly, I heard my name called, and I looked up to see Alyson and Glenn, Earl and Harriet running toward me. Earl picked Kathy up and swung her up on his shoulders. They were all laughing as I was crying. Alyson said that they had been in prayer for Kathy and God told them to come home. She said, "Betty, he said you needed us." Earl beamed at me and said, "Kathryn Kuhlman is going to pray for this child today even if I have to carry this baby up to her in the middle of the service!"

Earl didn't have to, because God beat him to it. The service had just begun, when Kathryn stopped everything and said, "There is a child here that Jesus wants to touch." She came down from the platform and headed straight for Kathy. Kathy was standing in front of me, putting little candies in the element cup on the back of the pew in front of us. I had brought the candy to keep her content during the service. She didn't even notice Kathryn approaching her. Kathryn reached out, put her hand on Kathy's head and said, "The power of the Lord is on this child." Kathy gave a scream and was knocked to the floor. Power like an electrical shock surged from Kathy, through me, and into the arm of Harriet Mason, who had her arm around my shoulder. She wasn't able to use her arm for the rest of the day.

I didn't know what had happened to Kathy. I tried to pick her up, but she was as limp as a dishrag. Earl and Glenn finally got her up and laid her across our laps. I have a hard time describing what she looked like. On her face there was confusion, but even more than that, there was wonder. It was as if she was in another place. We didn't know what the Lord did, but I knew Jesus had touched my child.

For years, I wondered what happened to Kathy that day. Outwardly she wasn't healed. She is twenty-three now and is only about two or three mentally. She needs constant care, which I will lovingly give her until the day I die. Then her sister, Laurie, will take over.

But Kathy has given this family something a regular child cannot give. She has taught us lessons we would not have learned without her. She has been a trial for my patience sometimes, and the reason for my existence at others. She can be an exasperating terrible two year old at one moment, and my perpetual baby the next. Because of Kathy, I have learned what life is really all about. It isn't the pursuit of money and fame. It is the satisfaction of loving and being loved in return. It isn't the greed of grasping and taking. It is the joy of giving and sacrificing. She has shown me the shallowness of my soul, and how much I can expand it with the love of Jesus.

I remember taking part in one of the field trips conducted by Kathy's special school. We all went out on a boat, touring the marina around Balboa and Newport Beach. It was a beautiful sunshiny day, and the children were really enjoying themselves. I marveled at the patience of the teachers, who had devoted their lives to these special children. I was having a hard time because it was so hard for me to look at the other children with the same kind of love I had for my own daughter.

Kathy is a beautiful child. Because she was not born retarded, we have been blessed with a perfectly normal looking girl. She is as neat as a pin, and eats beautifully, with excellent table manners. Anyone casually observing Kathy, when we take her out to a restaurant, would not realize that she has a problem.

This was not the case with most of Kathy's classmates. Some of these children are very sad to look at. My heart went out to them, but after a day of watching those wonderful teachers try to feed mouths that couldn't handle food, wipe faces that would stay dirty without help, and sponge down clothes that were disaster areas, all I wanted was to get out of there. I wanted to take my pretty little daughter home, put her in her comfortable bed, and forget there was such agony in this world. The shallowness of my spirit was appalling to me, but I couldn't control my feelings.

When the boat neared the dock I was leaping for joy inside at seeing the end of the trip, yet dying of shame at the same time for my poor attitude. I was praying that none of those devoted teachers would be aware of what a terrible person I was. Quickly I hurried Kathy back on the bus and gave a sigh of relief. At last we were on our way home. But I was not going to get off that easily, because matters got worse.

Suddenly, one of the bigger girls gave a scream and began to thrash and kick. She was yelling and screaming, flailing her arms about, and stamping her feet. Finally she managed to kick a window out of the bus. My mind was in a state of shock, taking in this terrible scene. The girl was not only severly retarded, she was also blind. Her only security was her mother and she had not been able to come with us that day. The exhaustion of the day, not being able to see where she was, and the new surroundings were too much for the child to handle and she literally exploded.

The only way the teachers could handle her was to man-handle her into submission before she could hurt herself. She made me think of a frightened wild animal, cornered with no place to turn.

My mind was screaming, "*LET ME OUT OF HERE!*" I prayed I wouldn't panic. Then I looked down at my little girl. With all the love that is wrapped up in her little body, she was reaching out to this hurting child. Kathy began to pat and calm her. She stroked her leg and caressed her arm, and babbled, in her limited vocabulary, words of comfort. At that moment I came alive. The lack of love and compassion that had held me in bondage all that day left me, as I plugged into the love of Jesus for this child.

It was with his love that I reached out and took this child in my arms. It was with his love that I cradled this hurting lamb in my lap all the way back to the school. It was with his love and compassion that I was able to soothe to sleep this little one, until she was like a dove nestled in the circle of my arms, out of danger and free of fear.

It was also his love that Kathy demonstrated with her pats and caresses, that opened the floodgates of affection, that flowed with their healing power over this child. No, I don't know what happened to Kathy that day with Kathryn Kuhlman, but I will take her and love her exactly as she is. I know that I am the luckiest of all mothers.

CHAPTER 10

The Tarnished Ministry

The Christian Center Church was sold and our congregation moved into Melodyland Theater, a large entertainment arena in Anaheim, in 1969. Our church attendence had gotten to the point that it took five services on Sunday to accommodate everyone. If we were to continue growing, Melodyland Theater would meet all of our needs.

I was filled with trepidation about the move. I know the Spirit of God moves with his people, but I was so used to the intimacy of this little church. I was afraid that the huge Melodyland arena would never feel the same. It had been a theater in-the-round and could seat over 3,000 people in the main auditorium.

Things changed there, at least for me. What I had experienced at Christian Center I never experienced at Melodyland (now called Melodyland Christian Center). Never again would I feel the same flowing of the Spirit, as God's people sang to him in his heavenly language that only he understood. After we moved to Melodyland, Pastor Ralph Wilkerson decided that he didn't want to offend anyone visiting, so he eliminated such "singing in the Spirit" from the church. It's funny, even when I had been a visitor, the free flowing, sweet Spirit of God was the hook Jesus used to capture my heart.

Michael was delighted with the new church facilities. He had a huge conference room in which to teach his class, and more and more people came every Sunday. He now wanted Pastor Ralph to ordain him at the next Charismatic Clinic. He improved his behavior at home in anticipation of this new position in the church.

There was one thing that happened at about this time that still leaves me puzzled. Mike and I were sitting together during a service at Melodyland. Suddenly Pastor Ralph referred to Mike and pointed him out in the audience. He then proceeded to tell everyone that Michael was a former rabbi, who now had found his Messiah. I knew this wasn't the truth! Mike had never been a rabbi! I turned to Mike, and started to say something to him, but he hastily motioned for me to be quiet.

When we got home, I really started asking questions. The first one was, "Did you tell Ralph you were a rabbi?" Mike swore that he hadn't told him anything like that. I asked, "Well where in the world would he get an idea like this?" The only thing that Mike could think of was that he had told Ralph that he had some rabbinical training, and Ralph had decided to capitalize on this. Mike told me that he thought Ralph was an opportunist and that when he saw something he knew would excite the people, he would jump on it immediately, true or not. I never found out whether Mike told this story to Ralph or if Ralph made it up, but I do know that from that day forward Mike became Ralph's resident rabbi, and was constantly introduced in this manner.

In the years to come this description that I foolishly let slide proved to be a constant problem. The first problem came when Logos Publishers contacted Mike and wanted to do a book on his testimony. After all, he was the only orthodox rabbi in the country to become a Christian. Mike tried to get me to write his story for him, but I said I wanted no part of it. I knew it was going to be filled with lies. Finally he sat down and wrote out a few pages and sent them in to Logos to see if it was what they wanted. He received a quick reply. They suggested Mike obtain a ghost writer. He seemed to be unable to put any emotion down on paper.

Mike didn't have the slightest idea how to find a ghost writer, so he started working on me again. He would start first thing in the morning and not stop until we went to bed at night. I got all the arguments he could possibly think of, and I kept refusing. I told him that I would have to incorporate so many lies into his story to cover for the lies he was already telling, that I wouldn't know where to start.

It soon became obvious that he had no intention of getting off my back until I agreed. So, reluctantly, I said I would write it for him. I told him the only way I could approach it was as if I were writing fiction. That is exactly how I wrote it. The only true feelings that I put down were my own, when I wrote about the children.

I tried to forget I was Mike's wife. I would interview him, and write what he told me as if he were a stranger. It soon became obvious why he couldn't write about his emotions: he didn't have any. I would have to picture how I would feel in any given instance, and write that down as if that were how he felt. Every time I asked him, "Well, how did you feel about that, Mike?" I would always get this blank look: he didn't feel anything.

I knew it then and I know it now: I never should have let Mike talk me into doing this. The sin of writing this book will always have its repercussions. There will be copies around for years to come, and the people who read it may hear the truth about Mike and think that Jesus is as phony as the book. Of all the sins I have committed since I became a Christian, this one stands at the top of the list. The blurb, *A Rabbi Meets His Messiah*, printed on the cover of *Michael, Michael, Why Do You Hate Me?* is a constant reminder of my failure to stand up for the truth. I will never stop asking God and his people for forgiveness of this sin.

From that point on I absolutely refused to write another book for Mike. Since he was unable to write for himself, his publisher got him a beautiful ghost writer, Irene Harrell. Irene wrote from Michael's teaching tapes and she did a wonderful job. Irene did not know he was lying on his tapes, so she was able to write with a clear conscience. One good thing was that Mike never lied about the scriptures or changed them to suit his life style. His personal life was where all the falsehoods abounded.

Another time the rabbinical label proved to be a millstone around Michael's neck was at Melodyland Christian Center itself. The problem started when Melodyland started as a seminary. Dr. J. Rodman Willams was brought in as its president. Dr. Willams was a highly respected man in the field of education, so it was expected that his teaching staff would consist of nothing but high quality teachers.

Dr. Willams was told about Michael Esses, who was an orthodox Jewish rabbi, now a born-again Christian, and head of the layman's school, Melodyland School of the Bible. Dr. Willams was aware of the comprehensive education that went into rabbinical training, so Michael seemed a perfect candidate for his staff. He invited Michael to teach Hebrew in the seminary, called the Melodyland School of Theology.

The school applied for accreditation and in order to pass the scrutiny of the accreditation committee, the teachers had to have degrees. Dr. Willams asked Michael for a copy of his degree, so it could be added to the school files. Since Mike hadn't even finished high school, where in the world was he going to get a degree?

He came up with two different schemes. The first was the easiest, he only had to come up with some ordination papers. So he printed up a blank certificate and filled it in.

First he put the words *The Sephardic Yeshiva of N.Y.* at the top of the certificate. These words were bisected with a star of David with Hebrew lettering in its middle. Under the star were the words *Certificate of Ordination.* Following is a reproduction of the entire certificate.

THE SEPHARDIC   YESHIVA OF N.Y.

CERTIFICATE OF ORDINATION

This Is To Certify: That *Michael Isaiah Esses*

having proved his DIVINE GIFT and calling according to the WORD of GOD, and having completed fourteen years in the study of THE TORAH and twelve years in the study of THE TALMUD, and having met the standards of THE SEPHARDIC YESHIVA of NEW YORK, and as prescribed by its ARTICLES of INCORPORATION of THE STATE of NEW YORK, has on this ___30___ day of ___June 1950___ by the laying on of hands and prayers of the board of RABBIS been set apart and ordained as a RABBI, conferring upon him THE DOCTORATE of HEBREW LETTERS, and the right to

Preach and Teach The Torah and The Talmud

Administer the ordinances of the SYNAGOGUE, perform the RITE of MARRIAGE, BURY THE DEAD, and FEED THE FLOCK of GOD.

IN WITNESS WHEREOF, the EXECUTIVE OFFICERS of THE SEPHARDIC YESHIVA of NEW YORK, of KINGS COUNTY, NEW YORK at 2169 - 67th Street, BROOKLYN, NEW YORK have set their hands and seal.

This ___30___ day of ___June 1950___

CHIEF RABBI AND PRESIDENT

SECRETARY

THIS IS TO CERTIFY :)   18/95   X56

THAT

HAVING PROVED HIS DIVINE GIFT AND CALLING
ACCORDING TO THE WORD OF GOD, AND HAVING
COMPLETED FOURTEEN YEARS IN THE STUDY
OF THE TORAH AND TWELVE YEARS IN THE
STUDY OF THE TALMUD, AND HAVING MET
THE STANDARDS OF THE SEPHARDIC YESHIVA
OF NEW YORK, AND AS PRESCRIBED BY ITS
ARTICLES OF INCORPORATION OF THE STATE OF
NEW YORK, HAS ON THIS _____
DAY OF _____ 12 may (for month and year)
BY THE LAYING ON OF HANDS AND PRAYERS OF
THE BOARD OF RABBI'S BEEN SET APART AND
ORDAINED AS A RABBI, CONFERRING UPON HIM
THE DOCTORATE OF HEBREW LETTERS, AND THE
RIGHT TO
    PREACH AND TEACH
    THE TORAH AND THE TALMUD
ADMINISTER THE ORDINANCES OF THE SYNAGOGUE,
PERFORM THE RITE OF MARRIGE, BURY THE DEAD,

The above is Mike's hand written copy of his ordination certificate that he gave to the printer.

PAUL R. WEAST

MASTER CERTIFIED GRAPHOANALYST

MEMBER BY INVITATION

13731 LINDALE LANE
SANTA ANA, CA 92705
(714) 544-9240
(714) 669-1421

TO WHOM IT MAY CONCERN

I, Paul R. Weast, Master Certified Graphoanalyst and
Handwriting Identification Expert, declare I have carefully examined and made detailed comparisons of the
cursive and printed handwriting on the following documents:

1. CERTIFICATE OF ORDINATION of Michael Isaiah Esses,
dated 30 ,June, 1950 and identified as Exhibit A.

2. A legal size sheet of paper bearing the printed text in
a word for word model of the printed CERTIFICATE OF
ORDINATION. This document also contains handwritten notes
in cursive writing. It is identified as Exhibit S-1 .

3. A letter on Town Drapery Center letterhead, dated 8-8-65.
It is signed Michael. It is identified as Exhibit S-2.

4. Nine (9) cancelled checks, drawn of the Union Bank,
Orange, Ca. and each signed Rev. Dr. Michael Esses. These
are collectively identified as Exhibit S-3.

It is my professional opinion that the handwriting, both
printed and written that appears on each of these documents
were made by the same person.

Signed in Anaheim, California on June 11, 1983

Paul R. Weast

Paul R. Weast, MGA

QUESTIONED DOCUMENT EXAMINER   HANDWRITING ANALYSIS

**Notarized Graphoanalyst
report which confirms
that Michael wrote and
signed his own rab-
binical ordination.**

The certificate of ordination was printed at Associated Typographers in Anaheim, and the the corporate seal was made at Worthen Stamp and Seal, also in Anaheim. This was the certificate given to Dr. Williams to place in his files. A handwriting identification expert has examined this document and his conclusion is on the previous page.

The second plan was more complicated and cost a lot more money. He decided that if what they wanted were degrees, then he would get degrees. He went to a local private college and for several thousand dollars obtained a B.A., an M.A., and a Ph.D.

Moishe Rosen, who heads Jews for Jesus, an organization dedicated to evangelizing the Jewish people for the Lord, met Mike and then questioned him about his background. I don't know what it was that made Moishe skeptical of Mike, but he started investigating him. The first thing he did was to obtain a copy of Mike's rabbinical ordination from the Melodyland files.

Someone in Rosen's organization must have been a friend of Mike's, because she called and told Mike that Moishe had checked on his ordination papers, and was convinced they were phony. The person who called said, "I think Moishe is going to expose you, so you better get in touch with him to see if you can't clear this matter up." Of course, Mike assured the caller that there had been a terrible mistake which would be rectified immediately, and thanked her for calling him.

I was hard-pressed not to start saying, "I told you so," because I had warned him over and over that he was playing with fire. He would always tell me the same thing: "Shut up, and mind your own business." So, I just listened to him yell, and finally when he calmed down, I said, "Mike, why don't you call Mr. Rosen and see what he says to you."

I didn't hear the subsequent telephone converstion, but Mike told me that Moishe told him that he had checked New York and discovered there was no Yeshiva in New York that could have issued Mike's ordination. Mike, of course, insisted to Moishe that it had existed at one time, and that he would send him proof of that fact. He had to buy time.

For the next few days Mike was like a caged lion, pacing back and forth, trying to figure out what he was going to do. Finally he decided to go talk to Walter Martin. Walter taught in the Melodyland School of the Bible and School of Theology and enjoyed a worldwide reputation as an expert in cults and world religions. He was also known as a man of integrity. I didn't know the man except in passing, but I couldn't imagine what Mike was going to tell him, in order to get him to help him.

Walter hadn't been at Melodyland very long, so there was no reason for him to doubt Michael's sincerity, or his credentials. After all, Michael was president of the School of the Bible, and had held that position for years. Walter knew he was a knowledgable teacher and that he was respected in the church. The story Michael gave Walter was that Moishe Rosen was going to ruin him because he mistakenly thought Mike's ordination was not authentic, as Mike had never attended a Jewish university.

Mike explained to Walter that the Judean Jews were such a minority of the Jewish people that they had their own schools for their rabbis incorporated right in their synagogues. He told him that his customs were as different from Moishe Rosen's people as day was from night. He told him that he couldn't make Moishe understand that his people didn't go to the universities like Moishe's people. He also told him that the synagogue where he was taught had closed years before, and he didn't know how to prove it had existed. Then, he asked the big question: "How do I handle this?"

Walter told Mike that he would think about it and see if he couldn't come up with something that might help. (Remember Walter didn't know the truth.)

Walter talked to Pastor Allen Porterfield about Mike's problem. Allen was pastor of a Southern Baptist church in a neighboring city. He also knew Michael well, since Mike taught a class in Allen's church one night a week. These two men discussed the possibility of nominating Michael for ordination in the Baptist church. This was the same ordination that Moishe held and they thought Moishe might be satisfied with his own denomination's ordination of Mike.

When Mike told me how these men were trying to help him, I couldn't help but reflect back to that Sunday morning when Pastor Wilkerson had first opened his mouth and started this whole mess. I wished I had run up on the platform at that moment, and yelled, *"THIS MAN IS NOT AND NEVER WAS A RABBI!"* It is bad enough to base one's own ministry on a lie, but to involve other innocent peoples' ministries is a terrible thing to do. I was so ashamed of Mike, that I at first refused to go to the ordination, but Mike didn't let me get away with it. Under protest I watched Mike become an ordained Southern Baptist minister. Pastor Allen helped Mike draft the following letter to Moishe Rosen on October 28, 1975. Neither Allen nor Walter knew they were covering fraud.

Dear Moishe,

Pursuant to our last conversation and to your inquiries regarding my rabbinical credentials, I will be sending you verification of my background and training as a Sephardic Rabbi within the next 30 days. I am currently completing research in the area of Sephardic Yeshiva and am seeking verification of my credntials through an agency which I am sure will satisfy you since it is internationally known and respected in the Evangelical world. If you will bear with me over the next month I think you will be quite satisfied with the outcome.

With much appreciation for your patience and cooperation I remain yours in Christian Fellowship.

Michael Esses

Of course, the agency alluded to in this letter was the Southern Baptist Church. Moishe Rosen was to assume that this church would never ordain Michael if his credentials weren't authentic. The verification that Moishe Rosen received was a copy of Mike's Southern Baptist ordination.

There is a postscript to this story. After Mike left us, I talked to Moishe Rosen. We spoke about the fact that Mike was an imposter. Moishe said, "Betty, I always knew Mike was a phony. He made one mistake that tripped him up. When he made the seal that he used on the certificate, he put on it that Yeshiva was incorporated in New York. All I had to do was check the records of incorporation, to find out it never existed."

He also told me that he had never intended to expose Mike, mostly because of the damage it could do to his own ministry. He said that he didn't need the hurdle of Mike's deception in his way when he witnessed to the Jewish people: "They would call us all a bunch of phonies, and if we declared our sincerity, they would ask us, 'How about Michael Esses?' " Moishe said the only thing that he always made sure of was that he never shared the same platform with Mike.

CHAPTER 11

The Work Of God
& The Work Of Man

By this time, Melodyland Christian Center had become the focal point of all of our activities. Over the years our involvement at Pastor Wilkerson's church had multiplied tremendously. When we first went into the huge new building, it seemed to swallow the congregation that had spilled out the sides of the original Anaheim Christian Center. It was decided that we would curtain off some of the auditorium so that people wouldn't have to spend the service staring at empty seats across the circular stage. Mike ran our drapery business, so he supplied the draperies for bisecting the circular church right down the middle. It didn't take too long for the curtains to come down, because the church was growing at such a rapid pace.

Pastor Ralph Wilkerson kept the format that had proven so successful at the original Christian Center. He preached in the Sunday morning service, and usually brought guest speakers in for the evening service. These speakers came from all over the country and were in the forefront of the charismatic movement. The names of David du Plessis, Pat Robertson, David Wilkerson, Charles and Francis Hunter, George Otis, Pat and Shirley Boone, Mario Murillo, Nora Lam, Dennis Bennett, Hal Lindsey, Oral Roberts, Ruth Carter Stapleton, Gene Scott, Rex Humbard, Charles Simpson, John Olsteen, Derek Prince, Bob Mumford, Brother Andrew, Corrie ten Boom, Jim Bakker, and Maria Von Trapp all graced the marquee outside Melodyland.

Melodyland has been from the beginning the showplace of the charismatic movement. The facility itself contributed to this image, because of its theatrical beginning. Many bright stars of stage and screen played this theater while it was a flourishing showplace, so it seemed only natural that the "stars" of the charismatic movement would trod its boards when it became a center for Christians.

Melodyland was a success. We were packed out every Sunday. We enjoyed a nationwide reputation as a great center for the charismatic movement, and our business neighbors, who had been so skeptical of us in the beginning, decided they had been a bit hasty in their judgement. Melodyland was a church you could support with a great deal of pride and devotion.

Melodyland had become world famous for its annual summer Charismatic Clinics, week-long conferences uniting charismatic Christians from around the world for Bible study, fellowship, teaching and mutual edification. Pastor Wilkerson always held the Christian Center ordination service during the Clinics: He believed that those who were to be ordained as ministers to the people of God could thus receive the special blessings of Christians from around the world. Two clinics had been held at Melodyland when Anaheim Christian Center rented the then secular facilities. August of 1970 would be the first time *Melodyland* Christian Center would offer Melodyland as its home for the Clinic.

I knew how badly Michael wanted to be ordained then. He was giving Ralph no rest on the subject. Finally Pastor Wilkerson asked our friend, Bob DeBlase, what he thought about the idea of ordaining Mike at that summer's Clinic. Bob and his wife, Marie, had been at Christian Center for years, since there had been only about 150 members. During the first few years of Christian Center, Bob and Pastor Wilkerson often celebrated their birthdays together. Ralph and his wife Allene enjoyed many meals at the DeBlase home. Marie was a superb Italian cook. This first time Pastor had asked Bob about Mike, Bob knew that Mike was involved with another woman, and that it was causing a lot of heartache in his home. So he told Pastor Wilkerson Mike was not ready for ordination: his home was in a shambles. He told Pastor that he should chastise Mike, not ordain him. I don't know whether Pastor Ralph took Bob's advice to chastise Mike or not, but it was shortly after this that Mike began to change at home. He quit staying out late, and he started treating us like family instead of enemies.

Later, Pastor called Bob into his office and again asked him: "Do you think Michael is ready for ordination?" Bob told him that Mike *seemed* to be trying to mend fences at home, but that Bob was still concerned. But I guess the pressure Michael brought to bear on Ralph was too much, because Pastor finally agreed to ordain him at the 1970 Charismatic Clinic. When Mike told me that this year's Clinic would end with the usual ordination service, and that he would be one of the candidates for ordination, I had very mixed emotions. I didn't know whether to be happy or to be sad.

Only someone who has lived with a spouse who is chronically unfaithful can tell you how "we live in hope and die in despair," as the old saying goes. There is something inside—maybe your pride, your hope, or your only means of survival that closes your eyes to the fact that you are married to a perpetual womanizer. Sometimes this almost unreasonable optimism is caused by the counseling you get from well-meaning people, whose idea of marriage counseling is one of shared complicity. In other words, if you have problems in your marriage, you both share in the guilt and the responsibility equally. But sometimes this is just not true. Sometimes your mate has a problem that did not begin with you and has nothing to do with you. The real complicity on my part was that I continued to maintain silence even in the face of Mike's deception. Inadvertantly, I was helping him to sin.

A lot of men who fit into Michael's category share a problem. Their hangup is not sex: it is adoration. Mike even would tell his girlfriends that his sex life at home was quite satisfactory. That wasn't his problem. What he needed was blind adoration from women who really didn't know him. As soon as they became aware of his shortcomings, the affair was over. It was necessary for him to be viewed by his latest love as perfect. Marriage quickly alerts lovers to the mate's imperfections.

Because of how he lived his life, when I first heard that Mike was going to be ordained, all I could think was that this was as wrong as it could be. My idea of an ordained minister was one who had proved he had the call of God upon his life by living righteously before others. I knew that the man who was anointed to be a servant of God should have submission to Jesus at the core of his being, and his personal life sould be in harmony with that submission. This was certainly not the case with Mike. He had just ended one affair, and I didn't know how long it would be before the next one would come along.

On the other hand, I couldn't help wondering if maybe the honor of being a "man of God," officially ordained by Melodyland, might not give him the inspiration needed to commit totally to God and straighten out his life. I knew that Ralph was aware of the women in his life, so if he had agreed to ordain Mike, maybe he could see something that I wasn't able to see because of my previous hurt and disappointment.

It was on a hot night in August in Anaheim that Michael was ordained a minister of the gospel from Melodyland, anointed in the service of the Lord. I will not attempt to tell you what was written across the faces of knowing family and friends at this occasion. That evening at the party I threw for Michael honoring his ordination, I saw Michael slip away and head upstairs. I followed him and stood at the top of the stairs, where I could hear him on the phone. He was calling his current girlfriend and telling her how much he loved her and how much he wished she could have been at the church to share this wonderful evening with him.

I should have been given an Oscar for my performance the rest of the evening. It seemed to me that all my prayers for this man were bouncing off the ceiling, never to be heard by God. It was so discouraging, watching everyone congratulate Mike, while he beamed back at them with the innocent face of a new-born baby. After everyone went home, I sat down and told Mike that I had heard him on the phone to his girlfriend. His first tactic was always to go on the offensive when cornered. I was immediately read the riot act for eavesdropping. Then Mike told me that he had tried to get rid of her before his ordination, but she told him that she would tell her husband about the affair if he had dared cut her off.

She and her husband had already broken up, and she had moved out with her kids. Apparently the husband didn't care if she left, as long as Mike had nothing to do with it. He was supposed to have told her that if Mike Esses was involved then both she and Mike were dead. Now, Mike said she was blackmailing him into staying with their relationship, and she had Mike paying for all of her expenses now that she was alone.

I could not believe I was having this conversation with a man who had been ordained that very evening. I felt every bit as trapped as Mike was saying he was. The only thing I finally managed to choke out, through clenched teeth, was, "You had better find a solution to your problem fast, or what this woman is putting you through will be a picnic compared to what I will do!" I was so angry, I nearly took the door off its hinges when I slammed the bedroom door and locked it against Mike.

I thought that night would never end. My anger was eroded slowly through sleepless tossing and turning. By morning I was no longer angry. I was resolute about standing firm against Mike and his "explanations." Only my tears revealed my inner agony as I emerged from the bedroom to face my unfaithful husband. Through tight lips I ordered him from my life: "It's over. I want you to leave." Mike started to plead with me, but I cut him off sharply. "You've gone too far. How can you stand up in that church and be ordained a minister of the gospel, in front of God and other Christians, while you are in the middle of an adulterous affair?"

Mike didn't even try to answer me. He knew I was ready to stand behind my order for him to leave. The only way he could salvage his position was to play his hidden card. Mike knew my most vulnerable spot, and he struck hard and fast. With a face full of sorrow and a voice trembling with emotion,he called the children into the room. With arms outstreched to them, he told them, "Your mother is throwing me out. I love you all so much. I don't know what I'll do without you. I'll probably never see any of you again." His voice broke, and he struggled to continue, "Please remember that I'll always love you. Please remember I tried to stay. Please say you'll still love me when I'm gone..." Mike's voice trailed off as he broke down again. John and Laurie looked at me in horror and threw themselves on Mike, begging him to stay. Mike continued with his drama, working the two children into an absolute frenzy over his leaving. He cried, he vowed undying love for them, he told them no matter how far away he had to go, he would never forget them.

By this time John and Laurie were completely hysterical. They turned from Mike and threw themselves on me, begging me to give their daddy another chance. As they clung to me, sobbing over losing their daddy, I looked over their heads toward Mike. His expression had transformed from sorrow to smiling triumph. His eyes challenged me to order him out in front of the children. I couldn't. He had won.

I'm sure I'm not the only wronged wife who has taken back an errant husband because of the children, but that afternoon I felt more alone than at any time in my life. Those who wonder how or why I could have put up with Mike for so many years and even have covered for him have never seen or heard children hysterical over losing their father. No matter what he did to me, Mike was still *Daddy* to them. I lived to regret surrendering to Mike's emotional blackmail, but it seemed like the only thing I could do. Mike realized that and used the same tactic on me time after time through the following years. I surrendered for the sake of my children. Unfortunately, my children ended up paying the price anyway through the emotional scars of a childhood full of manipulation and exploitation.

A few days later, Mike came to me and said he had taken care of the problem. He had asked a friend of ours, Paul Roper, to listen in and tape the conversation he had with this woman. She then was told that the conversation was not only taped but had been overheard by someone who was willing to testify that she was trying to extort money. She was told that if she persisted with what she was doing, she would end up in jail. I asked Paul if this was true, and he just said: "Betty, you don't have to worry about this woman again."

I think Mike realized I was at the end of my rope, because his whole attitude changed toward me. He began wooing me again, like he had done before we were married. But it was not doing much good, because I could hardly bear to look at him, much less resume marital relations with him. When I went to Pastor Wilkerson for counseling, he told me I needed to give Mike a chance to prove himself, that I had to forgive him because he was, somehow, repentant. So, once again, I was set up for the next blow.

This betrayal didn't come for the next couple of years, but in the meantime I found out why Ralph had always been so lenient.

We were in Israel. It was our third trip and this time Mike was even the co-leader of the tour. We were responsible for keeping track of the people on the trip. On this particular night a couple of the teenage girls on the tour had gone out and had not returned, and it was well past midnight. Mike looked exhausted and I knew he had a hard day coming up, so I told him to go on and go to bed, that I would wait up for the girls.

I was sitting in the lobby of the hotel, drinking coffee and reading a magazine, trying to keep myself awake, when one of the members of the tour appeared in the door. It was Mahlon Mc-Courry. I waved him over to ask him if he had seen the girls. Mahlon said he hadn't seen any of our people. He had just been out walking.

Mahlon attended Melodyland and was a quiet, very nice man who taught school in the Anahiem high school district. This night he was very troubled. As he sat there, I realized that he had tears in his eyes, so I asked him if he wanted to talk. He was reluctant, at first, to say anything to me, but finally he said what was troubling him. I was surprised at what he poured out to me next.

Mahlon was on the board of elders at Melodyland, and just prior to this trip to the Holy Land, a special meeting of this board was held. Apparently, Ralph had been having an affair with a young woman, and it was revealed to the council. My disbelief must have been mirrored in my face because Mahlon said, "It's true, Betty, Ralph confessed it was true and repented in front of the whole council!"

This was a terrible blow to Mahlon. He was trying desperately to get a handle on it. As I started to speak to him, he interrupted me with the words, "I thought so much of this man, it never occured to me that he could do something like this." Mahlon told me that he had been in the Navy, and had indulged in all the things sailors do. He said that once he had found Jesus, that kind of life was behind him, and he could never fall into those sins again. He just kept on saying, "I don't understand, I don't understand." It wasn't hard to tell that the man was heartbroken with disappointment.

My problem now, in that hotel lobby, was Mahlon. How could I help this man who had been so disillusioned? I asked the Lord to help me, and I said, "Mahlon, you know that Ralph came from a background where being naive was a way of life. His father was a preacher and all Ralph has ever known is church. He is not wise to the ways of the world like you, so it was easier for Satan to fool him than it would be to fool you. I imagine Ralph has learned a valuable lesson from this, and if Jesus can forgive him, I guess you'll have to, too."

Later I quietly slipped into bed, so I wouldn't waken Mike, and lay there, thinking about what I had heard. I was glad it was me that Mahlon had talked to, and not some of the other people on the tour. While I was surprised, I was not shocked. No one could have lived through as many other women as I had and continue to be shocked that these things happen. I knew that Mahlon had made the mistake that I have seen so many Christians make. He had made a hero out of a man who was not a hero. There is only one hero: his name is Jesus. When we get our eyes off him and on to man, we are always in for a rude awakening.

The next morning was when I made my mistake. I told Mike that the girls had gotten back safely, and that I had lectured them. Then I foolishly told him about my talk with Mahlon. I should have had my tongue cut out before I told him this, because from that day forward he justified every affair with, "Well, Pastor did it, so it can't be that bad!"

CHAPTER 12

Anointed For Profit

As time went on, Mike became more and more immersed in his ministry. He closed the drapery store so he could give all of his time to teaching and speaking. When I say *all* of his time, I mean *all* of his time. His autobiography had come out and invitations for speaking engagements came daily. This week Pittsburg, the next Atlanta, then Cleveland and Akron. Back to San Francisco, over to San Jose. And he also had to fly back to Anaheim every Sunday to teach his class at Melodyland. This kept up week after week, month after month, year after year.

Life was going on as usual at home, too. There were the children to care for, and I was writing my own book. I also had the full time job of taking Mike to, and meeting Mike at, Los Angeles International Airport.

One thing had me concerned, and that was the marriage of our good friends, Marie and Bob DeBlase. They had always had a very rocky marriage. It was too bad, since they were both such nice people. They seemed to bring out the worst in each other. They had known each other since childhood, and from the stories they told, they had started battling constantly that long ago. Before we even had known them they had gone to court for a divorce, but Bob had reconciled because their children were still small and he felt guilty about leaving them. Also, with their Catholic upbringing, divorce was almost impossible. Bob and Marie were such close friends that with Mike gone so much, they had practically become part of my family. They were the ones I turned to for companionship and support. I loved Marie like a sister, and Bob had practically become the man of our house. I found myself leaning more and more on Bob to fill Mike's shoes, because Mike was never home.

Bob and I, from the moment we met, had become the best of friends. We thought alike and were so compatible that we were like a pair of old comfortable shoes together. I knew that Marie resented this relationship, since she and Bob were always so much at odds, but she loved me, so she joined us as well as she could.

It became increasingly evident that Bob cared too much for me, to the extent that even Mike noticed it. Mike would tell me, "The man lights up when you are in the room." One day, when Bob was taking Mike to the airport, Mike turned to him and said, "You're in love with Betty, aren't you?" Bob answered carefully but honestly: "I just can't help feeling about her the way I do, but I would never touch her, or hurt your marriage in any way."

When Mike told me this I knew I had to give up these friends who meant so much to me. This was one of the hardest things I ever had to do. I loved them both so much, and yet because of it, years passed before I ever saw them again.

During the next few years, Mike and I saw very little of each other. After my book was published, I also started on speaking trips, something expected of all authors. You have to help promote the sales of your book. Because of this exposure, I found that the Lord had given me the ability to minister and speak, using my experiences and growth in the Lord to help others. Before long I was in nearly as much demand as Mike. I was being featured at many of the charismatic clinics across the country, and even as far away as Australia.

About the only times Mike and I were together for an extended period were when we conducted our annual tours to the Holy Land. These trips were more popular each year. Mike was a natural as tour leader. One of his biggest assets was that he spoke fluent Arabic. This is the prevailing language of the people tour leaders work and trade with in Israel. Unfortunately, Mike's desire for money made the tours become too much business.

Rampant materialism had already raised its ugly head in Mike's life back home. He was driving Cadillacs and buying more clothes then most men could wear in a lifetime. Only the best restaurants were good enough for him, and the hotels where he stayed had to be the finest. When I would protest this needless extravagance, he would tell me this was how all the evangelists lived, so he was not out of line. Besides, he would add, the churches at which he was ministering picked up most of the tab anyway. The sad thing about Mike's statement about other evangelists is that in some cases it is true. Many charismatic leaders will only go first class, and it is the churches that have to pay for their extravagant life styles. I wonder what the apostle Paul would think about their material demands? From what I have read in the New Testament, his accommodations often left something to be desired!

Well, Israel proved to be a mecca for making money for Mike. Not only did he get his percentage of the original price of the tour, he also had many sidelines going for him. If the people had pictures taken by a group photographer, Mike got a cut of the photographer's fee. If they paid to go on any of the side trips, Mike got a cut. Tour members were taken only to shops where Mike had made arrangements with the proprietors in advance for a cut of all sales. Even at the end of the tour, when a collection was taken for the drivers and local guides, Mike got a cut of that, too!

The one time I had to lead the tour on my own because Mike was in the hospital, I changed all these arrangements. The only profit he made from that trip was his percentage of the tour price. He was furious with me when I told him I hadn't made a profit from one thing in Israel. Unfortunately, Mike wasn't the only one doing it. Many of the leaders of the Holy Land tours make the same kinds of arrangements.

The volume of Mike's purchases during each trip to Israel was unbelievable. There were only two other people I knew who were more avid shoppers than Mike: Pastor Ralph and Allene Wilkerson. When the Wilkersons joined our tours, Mike spent his time bargaining for them for just about everything in sight. They bought jewelry, clothing, ornate Bibles, furs, etc. One year, on the way back home from the tour, they even detoured to Austria, just to buy china.

I don't know what causes so many Christian leaders to need so much opulence. Our family had always lived nicely, but now we lived in luxury. Before I knew it, there were two Mark V's parked in our driveway, a station wagon for our trips to Ensenada, an RX7 Mazda for Laurie, and a van for John. Five cars in one family! The insurance premiums alone were enough to give me a heart attack!

What Mike refused to express in actions or words, he tried to prove to his children with lavish gifts. John would come home from lunch with Dad wearing an expensive new watch on his wrist. Laurie would come home from being with Mike with a new leather jacket or a new gold necklace, or anything else her heart desired. I would protest to Mike that he wasn't teaching them any values. He said they would learn that success was value enough.

At Christmas you would have thought Santa Claus stumbled and everything he was going to give to all of Anaheim had come tumbling down our chimney! I wouldn't get one diamond ring, I would find three of them under the tree. The presents I gave Mike, although always quite nice, looked totally inadequate compared to what he always gave me.

I could never get used to this extravagance. It was not how I had been raised. My people came from Texas, and most of my relatives are in the oil business, and several of them are millionaires. You would never know any of them had more than enough for a comfortable living. It would have been much too ostentatious for *any* of them to drive a Cadillac. I could never get used to all this display, although Mike tried to justify it to me and I tried for a while to live like he did. When I gave up, Mike *insisted* I play the show with him. He wasn't going to have anyone say his wife was shabby!

Ralph Wilkerson was also starting to live on a much grander scale than before. I could remember when we were still in the old Anaheim Christian Center and Mike and I put new draperies in the Wilkersons' bedroom, because the ones there were in tatters. Their home at that time was a modest tract house that showed the wear and tear of their growing children.

Now there was quite a change. Pastor appeared on the platform at Melodyland with one new suit after another. Allene wore nothing but designer clothes from stores like Nieman Marcus and Saks Fifth Avenue. Their home had gone from that simple tract house to a custom built home overlooking the ocean at exclusive Dana Point in southern Orange County. This million dollar home features sunken tubs, a sauna, gold plumbing fixtures, and a tree growing right up through the center courtyard. The furnishings are all antiques and custom-made furniture from Beverly Hills. There is a lovely guest house, and a swimming pool.

Pastor Wilkerson invested in two condominiums which were quite beautiful, and located on the beach in Oceanside (halfway to San Diego). Three different private planes were at their disposal, and Cadillacs and Lincolns became their means of transportation around town.

I was asked to speak one Sunday at the Melodyland branch church in Santa Barbara, two hours' drive north of Los Angeles. Allene Wilkerson flew in on one of the private planes to play the organ for the service. I didn't know it then, but she flew in every week to help with the services. Her daughter, Debbie, and son-in-law, Mike, were the pastors of the church. The Sunday I was there, the congregation consisted of only about twenty-five people. I think that if I had been in a decision-making role, I would have wanted to spend the Lord's money a little more prudently.

All of these things are contrary to what Jesus says should be important in our lives. I don't see how the people who preach and teach the word of God fail to get the message. I don't believe that Jesus wants us to ask for sacrificial offerings from people when we are living in opulence. I have known too many people who have given their last cent, and even gone into debt, to answer a rich evangelist's plea for more money.

Michael made a lot of money by appealing to Christians for special contributions. For example, after Proposition 13 was passed in California, Mike collected a lot of money from his 500 member Sunday School class by telling them that because of the cutbacks, his retarded daughter would probably be dropped from her state-supported special education classes. He told them how badly he felt that he couldn't afford to send her to private school, so she was just going to have to sit at home and vegetate.

Many of the wonderful people in his class came to his rescue. They began giving him money each month to pay for Kathy's *private* school. What these people never knew was that Kathy's special state-supported classes never closed and never were supposed to close. She still was going happily all those years. I didn't know anything about this scheme until years later, after Mike had already left us. I guess the people thought I knew they were helping my daughter.

One thing about this incident leaves me puzzled. Mike always drove to class driving a Mark V. He taught class with a four carat diamond ring on his finger, and the suit on his back cost at least $300-400. Couldn't these people see what was going on? Christians should guard themselves against such ministerial opportunism. Just because a man is ordained doesn't mean he can qualify for sainthood. He may have a lot of problems with his walk, and those problems can be spotted if you just open your eyes.

Gullibility is not the same as trust. All of us Christians have to smarten up. If we don't, there are no compelling reasons for men like Mike to straighten up their lives. We have given such "ministers" a license to steal with our blind, unquestioning loyalty. When I asked the person who told me about the school money why someone didn't challenge Mike, I was told that they didn't want "to touch the Lord's anointed." They said they felt it was up to God to deal with him.

I have researched the scriptures for the true interpretation of the phrase, "Don't touch the Lord's anointed." Every time I have found it in the Bible, it always refers to men that God anointed king. For example, David was not allowed to touch Saul because Saul was anointed king, not because he was a *minister*. Cyrus, king of Persia, and David, king of Israel, were also the anointed of God, and could not be touched *in their governmental positions*.

There have been many times when I was ministering for the Lord that I have anointed people. I have anointed commitments made to God. I have anointed people for healing. I have anointed a new house, a new car, and a new baby, all in the name of the Lord. But "the Lord's anointing" is a different anointing. The *Zondervan Bible Dictionary's* article on the subject can be summarized this way: David and Solomon were anointed, the oil symbolizing the Holy Spirit, and they were thus set apart and empowered for a particular work in the service of God. "The Lord's anointed" was the common term for a theocratic king.

The *Interpreter's Dictionary of the Bible* states that the theocratic character of anointment is also exemplified by the fact that the king was "The Lord's anointed," and a vassal of God who reigned in God's stead over his people. The title "The Lord's Anointed" was later shortened in Hebrew-Aramaic form to *Messiah*, and was translated into Greek as *Christ.*

As a result of my searching the scriptures, I can come to only one conclusion: "*The* anointing of the Lord" was held only by the kings and prophets of the Old Testament, and Jesus Christ in the New Testament.

We who are called Christians have *an* anointing by the infilling of the Holy Spirit. When we bring disgrace and ridicule upon the name of Jesus Christ by living lives of deception, corruption, avarice, and unfaithfulness, then we, *by our actions*, touch "The anointed of the Lord," Jesus Christ, and we will be dealt with accordingly by judgment. It is not in the *revealing* of sin that Jesus is touched, but it is in the *committing* of sin.

Some who have heard that I'm writing this book have told me that I'm touching the anointed of God, but my Bible tells me that they are wrong. I've tried hard not to judge and condemn, but merely state the facts as they have happened. My concern for the body of Christ is genuine, and my feeling of responsibility to help make that body become without spot or wrinkle is something I cannot dismiss. I'm aware that some will be hurt by seeing and hearing about the failings of popular Christian leaders, but refusing to reveal and *then deal scripturally* with the sinner only condones and perpetuates the sin. It does not urge the sinner to repentance and restoration. The truth sometimes hurts, but it is a healing pain that results in true Christian holiness.

Many sins have been overlooked and not dealt with because Christians were afraid of "touching the anointed of the Lord." Paul, the apostle, didn't pull his punches like that. He had read the Old Testament, too, but when he saw someone getting out of line, even if it was a fellow apostle, he didn't say, "I must not touch the Lord's anointed." His dealings with Peter in Galatians 2:11-14 certainly make this point. He told Peter to his face that he was blameworthy and that he stood condemned. He told him that he was not living up to the truth in the Bible, and in front of everybody, Paul challenged Peter for his hypocritical urging that the Gentiles should live like the Jews. If Paul were to stand up today in a church whose congregation had been sold the line "Don't touch the Lord's Anointed," he would be trampled to death by the "faithful" sheep before he could even finish his exhortation!

Matthew 18:15-17 tells us exactly what to do if our brother, even if he is a minister or evangelist, gets out of line. Matthew tells us to confront the person first. If he doesn't listen, take along two others, so you have witnesses to confirm what you have said. If he still doesn't listen, you should bring it before the congregation, and if he still doesn't listen, he should be put out of the church.

This is the formula laid out by the scriptures and this is the only formula that keeps the body of Christ pure and, most importantly, it is the formula that urges confession, encourages repentence, and begins restoration for the man who has broken his fellowshp with God by his sin.

CHAPTER 13

The Temptation

Melodyland was becoming more successful every year. The church was packed every Sunday and the School of Theology and Melodyland High School were both enjoying high enrollments and enthusiastic students. The August Charismatic Clinic had become an attraction for Christians throughout the country. Many Christians were scheduling their vacations around the clinic. Because of the many RVs and vans that were crowded into the parking lot during that week, Melodyland sometimes took on the appearance of a campsite. Everywhere Mike or I spoke, interest in Melodyland was remarkable. Melodyland was acclaimed by Christians all over the world as a shining example of the perfect charismatic church. But all was not perfect. Melodyland's financial status was in stark contrast to its glittering reputation. How could such a successful, popular church be such a financial disaster?

While we as a church were famous throughout the country for our services, our musicals, and our pastors, we were fast becoming infamous in our own community for not paying our bills. In fact, we owed practically every supplier in town. Whether the bills were for gasoline, hotel rooms, plumbers, books, building supplies, printing, office supplies or television time, they were not being paid. Our reputation for financial reliability with our regular creditors was bad, but it was even worse with the local banks.

It seemed as though Pastor Wilkerson was oblivious to what was happening. He was globe-trotting here and there all over the world. Between 1975 and 1978, the church financed his trips to Paris, Reno, Cairo, Kenya, Jerusalem, Zurich, Stockholm, St.

Moritz, Salzburg, Taiwan, London, Brussels, Rio de Janeiro, Guatemala, Honolulu, Caracas, Mexico, Tel Aviv, and Geneva.

Ralph was building the reputation of Melodyland across the globe, but at home it was beginning to crumble. You can only keep this kind of notoriety buried for so long, then the rumours begin to circulate even among your own people.

One thing that alerted people to the problem was the never-ending campaign to raise money. Whether it is in a local church or the so-called electronic church (television), when the emphasis is always on collecting money, something is wrong. If everytime you go to church the pastor spends a disproportionate amount of time telling you of his need for money, or everytime you tune in to your favorite T.V. evangelist, his subject is invariably about the finances of the ministry, something is wrong.

If every time that you listen to these men, they are talking about how Satan is attacking them through the media or other men, remember that God cleans up his own house. It might not be Satan at all. If the revelation of improprieties is upsetting them, just remember it was God who said that everything that is hidden will be revealed. If these men are having problems in this area, *God* may well be dealing with them, just like Micah reported on God's dealings with the leaders of Israel.

The pastor has to take responsibility for how the finances of his church are handled, especially in a church where he makes the major financial decisions. You'll never convince me that when God directs a man to build for him, that God would refuse to pay the bills. When this proves to be the case, then the minister in question is either way ahead of God or is listening to his own ego.

The way God works is shown in Exodus 12:36. God wanted something done that was going to cost a lot of money. He wanted to take all of his people out of Egypt and he knew this move had to be financed. After all, moving a whole nation from one place to another is a expensive proposition. Think of the funds that Congress would have to appropriate in order to move the entire population from one state to another!

God solved this problem for his people. He gave them favor in the eyes of the Egyptians and all the Israelites had to do was ask and they received. The Egyptians literally *stripped* themselves to finance God's project. Moses didn't have to spend his time browbeating his people for money. He didn't have to run a telethon or collect pledges. When God is in it, he moves on the heart of people, and the finances are supplied.

Mike's life was also going on with business as usual. Our home life was in chaos and the children now were teenagers who were becoming more and more aware of the hypocrisy in their home.

Mike would rail at John if he had the audacity to say he didn't like spinach. He would lecture him about the sin of hating *anything*. Then if one of the neighbor kids broke one of his sprinkler heads, Mike would be outside cussing and telling him if he saw them around his house again, he would shoot them. John would die of embarrassment at the behavior of his father toward his friends—especially because his friends knew his father was a minister.

Laurie was the typical new young teenager, starting to experiment with makeup and not always dressed as parents would like. But Mike's reaction, screaming scriptures interspersed with four letter words about Laurie looking like a harlot, only left her in a state of confusion.

Years later, in a revealing conversation I had with Laurie, she told me her childhood impression of the ministry. She said, "Mom, I knew Jesus from the time I was a little girl. I always knew he was real and he loved me. I also knew the Bible that Daddy and other ministers preached from was really the Word of God. But I didn't think the ministry was real. Daddy and those people like him weren't real. I looked at them as actors, just doing their jobs. At home they were who they *really* were. When they were in the public they were on stage, acting out their roles, reading their lines."

As usual when things were bad at home, another woman was entering the picture. One of Mike's staff volunteers, his most recent conquest, had called things off and Mike was looking for her replacement—but not to replace her staff talents.

Mike's volunteer had never gone to Israel, but Mike brought a little bit of Israel back to her in the form of a diamond cross and a sapphire ring surrounded by diamonds. I had seen these things when he bought them, but he told me they were for a man back home to give to his wife. Sometime later I was told that the volunteer had been the true recipient and was wearing them as a token of Michael's love for her.

I had known something was going on for some time, but I had gotten to the point where I just went about my life and tried not to let it hurt me any more. You can only be devastated so many times, and then you become immune to survive. I had so little respect for Mike by this time that nothing he did surprised me.

Mike's liaison was apparently well known among the staff at the church and Pastor finally made him replace his volunteer, because of the talk. She went to Lowell Jones, who worked at Melodyland, about a problem she had with Michael. Lowell told me about this visit after Mike and I were divorced. It seems that it was she who broke with Mike after being involved with him nearly four years. (I know she had some competition during at least some of this time.) Mike didn't want to let her go, so he told her he was going to commit suicide if she left him. She then heard he was in the hospital.

Mike was in the hospital about that time, but it was for his allergies, so she needn't have worried. But worried she was, so she asked Lowell to go to Mike and tell him that she still loved him, that the only reason she had broken with him was because she was under conviction of the Lord. I asked Lowell if he gave Mike the message. Lowell told me no, that it was just too embarrassing to talk to Mike about his mistress.

To keep myself busy, I accepted more and more speaking engagements. I had found a wonderful woman to watch my children, so I could leave without worrying about them. Lupe was a Christian, and gave my children as much love as they gave back to her. At times, I needed to get away from my situation at home, and to feel that I was at least worthwhile to others, even if Mike treated me so shabbily. An unfaithful husband can do terrible things to your self esteem.

I had help in my ministry, too, especially from my wonderful secretary and booking manager, Betsy Berg. Some of my staff was aware that I was having marital problems, but none of us ever talked about them. One of my helpers in particular seemed empathetic to my problems, and I appreciated his support over the months, even though I didn't reveal anything about Mike or his problems.

I knew this man was aware that something was terribly wrong with my marriage. He never said anything, but a trip the three of us made to Las Vegas must have confirmed what he already thought.

Mike and I were booked to speak at Cinerama Church in Las Vegas. After the meeting, Mike and I decided to take our helper to one of the late shows. He was a country boy and had never seen a big name entertainer, especially a singer, so we wanted to give him a treat.

We decided on Wayne Newton, but after we squeezed through all the people and were finally shown our table, Michael had a total fit. The table wasn't very good, but the temper tantrum that Mike threw was a lot worse. Finally, he stormed out, cussing the maitre d' every inch of the way. His language would have made a longshoreman blush, especially in public. We followed him out like a couple of little children, hoping against hope that the floor would open up and swallow us.

When we got outside, we just wanted to go back to the hotel, but Mike was on a roll. He said, "We're going to see a show or I'll know the reason why!" So he went into one hotel after another down the Las Vegas strip until he found a maitre d' who would let us in even though the show had already started.

Anne Murray was the singer, and she was very good, but it was hard to enjoy her because Mike was still acting so badly. At a late show like this the cover charge covers three drinks, so we first ordered cokes. Mike objected and ordered hard drinks for all of us.

When the two of us ignored the drinks that were served to us, Mike reached over and drank ours along with his own. Mike is so allergic to alcohol that he can't even use shaving lotion, so I knew he was really going to pay for this, but there was no way to stop him. I was right, because he was deathly sick the next day.

The man and I never discussed Mike's behavior. I was just glad that we had been booked into Albuquerque immediately after that so we could get away from Mike. Between his women and his miserable disposition he was really pushing me to the edge. I don't know how much longer I could stand it.

The Albuquerque meetings were tremendous and it was a great relief to be away from Mike. After one night, when they had combined the Full Gospel Businessmen and the Women's Aglow into one huge meeting, I was walking on air. We decided to get something to eat to wind down from the meeting.

Sitting there across from one another, eating hamburgers, we finally admitted that we really cared about each other. I'm not proud of this time in my life, but I was so hungry to hear a man tell me he loved me again that I didn't fight what happened. Neither of us had ever been unfaithful to our mates, but after months of working together, we had fallen for each other, and we didn't know what to do about it.

We had the next day free, so we decided to drive to Sante Fe. It was here that Mike finally ran us down by phone. He was like a madman. He was yelling and screaming, crying and begging me to come home. I told him that I had more meetings to go to, but he wouldn't hear of it. He told me either to come home on the next plane or he would come get me.

I knew what I had to do, though. I came back to California and the man and I arranged a time to talk. We talked it over and because of our commitment to the Lord, we made the decision never to see each other again. Neither one of us has ever broken this vow, even to this day.

I went to Pastor Ralph and told him what had happened. I also told him that I would have given anything if it hadn't happened, not only because of what I had done to the Lord, but because of what I had done to myself. I had forgotten what it felt like to be loved and respected and I didn't know how I could go back to what I had with Mike.

The next few months were very hard for me. Even when I ministered, all I could think of was how much better it would have been if he were there. Finally, time did its job and I was able to put it behind me. I sought the Lord's forgiveness and I received it. Keeping my vow and working hard on my marriage to Mike was my penance.

When I look back at this point in my life, it is with a combination of horror and sorrow. Horror that I could have stooped to the same level as Mike and committed adultery, and sorrow that now my children had to live with the fact that both parents had been unfaithful. The sin of covering for Michael and the unhappiness in our home had finally caught up with me and I paid the price by losing all the respect I had left for myself.

CHAPTER 14

The Moneychangers

The financial situation at Melodyland was rapidly deteriorating. The new multi-purpose building going up adjacent to the auditorium was a constant reminder of the insolvency of the church. This building had stood for years, half finished, while the funds to complete it were collected from the pulpit over and over again. Funds were collected for a wedding chapel again and again.

Funds were collected for carpeting for the Sunday School many times, until one of the teachers approached Pastor Wilkerson and demanded to know where the carpeting was for her children. Since she had contributed twice herself to this project, she felt she could ask.

Ralph turned to her and told her they hadn't gotten it yet because he had to pay the big bills. He showed her a bill for $5,000. When the woman said, "But Pastor, you weren't collecting money to pay that bill, you were collecting for the carpeting," Ralph's reply was very revealing. He said that he had to give the congregation a reason that would appeal to the people. Apparently children were appealing.

The money problem was so bad that the merchants in town didn't want to accept Melodyland checks anymore. All too often, they bounced skyhigh.

Lowell Jones, who worked at Melodyland, told me about the embarrassment of being taken to task each week at the Rotary Club meetings for the financial irresponsibility of Melodyland. He said some of the top local businessmen and city officials scolded him for the bad example that Melodyland was setting for the community. They said, "After all, Lowell, you people are supposed to be Christians setting a good example for the rest of us!"

They couldn't understand why Melodyland was constructing this new building when the people in town were not being paid their bills. Lowell said he couldn't reveal to them that many board members had objected to starting the new building when they couldn't meet the payroll, but Ralph had prevailed with the remark that those who objected had no faith.

Many people, especially those from a denominational background, cannot understand why the board of elders at Melodyland let Ralph Wilkerson run roughshod over them. Most of these men were competent businessmen who were well aware of the fact that you can't spend what you don't have. Yet, Ralph was running wild with TV shows, trips, elaborate musicals, building projects, charge accounts, etc. and it seemed there was no way to stop him, short of bankruptcy.

Why didn't the board stop Pastor Wilkerson? Why did they let him get in so deep? The answer is really quite simple. They *couldn't* stop him. In the first place, the by-laws of Melodyland stated that Ralph Wilkerson could not be replaced. This all by itself gave Ralph carte blanche for anything he wanted to do. In the second place, there were no place these men could go to appeal to authority.

Let me explain. If you are a Presbyterian and the board is having a hard time controlling the pastor, the elders can go to the synod of their district for help in the situation. This holds true for most demoninational churches. But if you were an elder of Melodyland, you had no place to go. You had two choices: agree with Ralph, or resign and go on down the road. This is a great pitfall of the independent church. It has to depend totally on the pastor to be the man of God that he should be. When you have the additional problem of everybody warning you not to touch the anointed of the Lord, you are up the creek without the well known paddle.

It was hard to believe that we could have gotten so far in debt. Melodyland wasn't a struggling, half-full church, with a congregation of uncommitted Christians who were just warming the pews on Sunday. You couldn't have asked for more involved, enthusiastic people for the Lord. A large percentage of them put their money where their hearts were and were devoted "tithers" in the church. If any church in this land should have been solvent, it was Melodyland.

Mike and I had been in touch with our friend, Paul Roper. He was living in Seattle and we had visited with Paul and his wife Cindy when we had been booked for a Full Gospel meeting in their city.

The years had been kind to Paul. He was an extremely successful businessman in Seattle who specialized in taking over businesses that were close to or in bankruptcy. These businesses were usually in this shape from mismanagement. Paul would come in and, through prudent management of the income, cutting out all unproductive drains on the business, and dismissing all personnel deemed unnecessary to the sucessful running of the business, would bring the company back to solvency.

When Mike and I returned home after the meeting in Seattle was over, Mike went to see Pastor Wilkerson. He told him about Paul and what he was capable of doing. Mike suggested that Ralph have a talk with Paul to see if Paul could help him with Melodyland.

Ralph must have been aware that he had pushed just as far as he could go. If something didn't happen to reverse the momentum, he would be bankrupt in no time at all. At any rate, Ralph agreed to talk to Paul to see if Paul could help him. I'm not sure why Paul accepted this job. It was probably partly the challenge, because Paul is the kind of man who loves a challenge, but I think he lived to regret the day Ralph Wilkerson turned to him for help.

Some of the facts that Paul had to face right off the bat were that the church was over eight million dollars in debt, there were twenty-six lawsuits pending against it, and it had been spending over two times its income for several years.

The Attorney General of the State of California was investigating the activities of an illegal trust fund, and part of the real estate was in foreclosure. There were people from the church who had obtained personal loans on their good credit, loans which Melodyland was supposed to repay at the bank, but these people were having to make payments themselves, because they were told there was no money. Many others had put their homes up as collateral for loans that Melodyland had obtained, and these homes were now in jeopardy.

Melodyland, and Ralph in particular, must have thought that Simon Legree in the form of Paul Roper had just hit town. Paul immediately put into effect the business practices that had proved sucessful in revitalizing many other floundering businesses.

The first thing he did was to pare down the personnel from 250 to 50 people. Many of these people were related to either Ralph or Allene. Melodyland had been rife with nepotism. Then he closed all the charge accounts, sold the three airplanes, the church in Santa Barbara, and all the T.V. equipment. Ralph's son-in-law would have to find a new place to preach.

His next big move was to make all the Melodyland outreaches self sufficent. This included the School of Theology, the High School, the School of the Bible, the Hotline, the bookstore, etc. In other words, if they couldn't pull their own weight, without help from the general fund of the church, then they had to close.

Cindy, Paul's wife, worked as his secretary and assistant, because she knew exactly how Paul handled things. It was her job to collect all the out-standing debts, list them, and make arrangements for monthly payments to the creditors. This proved to be quite a job, because there were drawers full of bills that had never even been opened.

The first few weeks, Paul and Cindy stayed with us, so I was aware of the mental and emotional strain that they were going through. Paul, despite his gruff exterior, has a soft heart, so it wasn't easy to dismiss all these employees. He knew some of them would have a hard time finding other positions. But for Melodyland to become financially sound, these things had to be done.

Ralph fought Paul every inch of the way. It became a daily battle for Paul to implement the necessary reforms. Every time Paul would turn his back, Ralph would break the rules. Paul would come home, sink in a chair, and say, "I wonder how many more bodies will rise to the surface before I can get back to that church tommorow."

Paul just couldn't stop Ralph from undermining him at every turn. For example, Ralph couldn't seem to understand that every time you take up a collection or a special offering for anything, you are taking money that would have been donated to the general fund that pays the bills. People have only so much set aside to give to the church, so when it goes in one direction it doesn't go in another. In other words, if you take a collection for a visiting ministry, or to send your son-in-law and daughter to China, or to finance a trip for yourself to evangelize Idi Amin, that money is gone and it is not replaced in the general fund to pay the bills. Ralph could not or *would* not understand. Ralph was not giving Melodyland's money to these projects, but the money that belonged to the trade people for jobs they had performed or merchandise they had supplied. The Bible says a worker is worthy of his hire, but this scripture seemed to be overlooked by Ralph.

Paul fought this battle every day, and I think it was only that he isn't the type of man who quits when the going gets rough, that kept him from saying, "I'm just going to give it all back, Ralph, you'll just have to sink by yourself!"

After a few months Paul had totally reversed the financial situation at Melodyland. Instead of spending two times our income, we now only were spending half our income. The outstanding bills were being repaid from the balance. This progress did not go unnoticed in our community.

CHAPTER 15

The Wise Counselor

"I know my husband is a psychological basketcase, but I'm not here about him. I want to know what is wrong with me that forces me to continue letting him treat me like I have no value." This was my opening statement to the psychologist I had agreed to see to try to find some answers to my problems.

The episode with our helper had an effect on me that went way beyond the brief encounter it was. It awoke in me an anger over my situation and how I was treated. I realized that I was so brainwashed and conditioned that I had gotten to the point where I was glad when another woman was in Mike's life, because it meant I would have a few good months when his affair was over, before the next one came along. I've heard of compensating, but this was ridiculous!

There comes a time in many people's lives when they need to recognize that they need help to find solutions to problems that slowly have been eroding their stability. If you are in a relationship that is slowly but surely destroying you, and you are unable to rise above the mire, then you need to reach out for some professional help.

You must be very selective about the professional help you seek. A strong recommendation from someone you know and respect is your first step toward getting constructive help. I know many people say that if you just trust God, you will never need professional help. Well, I trusted God to see that I found a professional counselor who could help me with my emotional needs just as I would pray for God's help in finding the right medical doctor for my physical needs.

Sometimes a person with problems only needs one or two sessions with a good counselor to gain the strength and perspective to work through some serious problems. Other times, the Lord may use one counselor to help you through extensive emotional and spiritual "rebuilding." Your own church is a good place to start looking for a good professional counselor. Don't settle for just anybody. Find someone who is well-trained, experienced, and whom you can trust to have your best interests at heart.

Dr. Bill Pickering proved to be the perfect psychologist for me. Walter Martin had recommended him to me, and his high estimation of the man proved to be correct. Dr. Pickering was a Christian psychologist whose approach was one of making a person feel good about himself. When you feel this way, you have the beginning of a good mental outlook on life. I realized I needed some professional help to sort out my life and get me on the road to peace and dignity that had escaped me for years.

I knew my attitude was changing at home, because I could no longer tolerate being treated with disdain. I loved Mike, or I wouldn't have stayed all those years, but I was having to face the question: do I love him enough to live this way the rest of my life?

We had been through so much together that a bond had been forged. My entire adult life had been lived with this man. Yet the commitment had really been one-sided. It was like I was married, but he wasn't. I had lived the life of a married woman. Mike had lived the life of a carefree bachelor.

After a few months with Dr. Pickering, I was able to see some of the areas where I had let distorted reasoning shape and mold my life. My main problem was feeling unreasonable guilt, and this is where I was in such a bad position with someone like Mike. I had too much conscience, and Mike didn't seem to let his conscience bother him.

Dr. Pickering was able to show me as the teenager who drifted into rebellion and finally went so far as to marry a man like Mike. He told me, "Betty, you knew that your parents were right about Mike. He was too old for you. He was too experienced for you. After all, he was a man who had fathered four children and you were only seventeen years old. Your parents recognized the fact that he was a man with little moral character, or his first family would not have been left behind. Yet, you married this man, in defiance of your parents' wishes. With your hyper cons-cience you were forced to make a total commitment to Mike in order to justify to your parents what you had done. You built yourself a prison from which there was no escape. Your parents' kindness and generosity throughout the years had the effect of freezing you into your position. After all, hadn't you rebelled against them, and given them a great deal of heartache? Instead of being mad at you, they were helping you make the best of things. So here is where the guilt set in. What did you think you deserved for your sin? Punishment. You've let Mike be your punishment all these years."

It was like a light bulb went on, because I was able to see what I had been doing to myself all these years. I stayed with Mike and accepted his treatment of me because I felt I deserved it!

Dr. Pickering asked me a very pertinent question during one of our sessions. He asked, "Betty, how much longer are you going to make that teenager pay for the mistake she made? Don't you think it's about time you let her off the hook?"

I didn't know what to answer him, because I thought he was telling me to leave my marriage, but that was not his position. He just wanted me to redefine and recognize how I had been living. He wanted me to quit compromising my conscience, which only intensified my guilt. He said, "You're going to have to quit lying for Mike, and covering for him. If he wants to live his life like that, then it's his problem. But you have to stop letting him involve you in it."

Then the doctor said the most healing thing he could have said. He told me that Jesus had died on the cross and paid for my rebellion with his life. Now I had to accept the fact that payment in full had been made, forgive myself, and to go on with my life.

How many times I had preached this message, but I had never applied it to my own life. Not only do we have to forgive others, we also have to forgive ourselves. So many of us messed up when we were teenagers, but the Lord doesn't want us to beat ourselves for the rest of our lives. He wants us to ask for forgiveness, accept forgiveness, and get on with it.

Mike would have had to be blind not to have seen the great growth and change in me over the next few months. I knew he was involved again, but this time I wouldn't cover for him, so he had to cover for himself. He did this by obtaining an answering service. From now on, if I wanted to talk to him or if anyone called, he had to be paged on his beeper. This way I didn't have to lie.

In January of 1979, I went into the hospital to have surgery. I knew, in my heart, that my marriage was over. The only thing missing was the final break. There was nothing in me that wanted to suffer anymore. I was looking clearly at Michael now. I knew he had loved me with all the capacity he had to love. I mourned for the love that we had at one time and for what it could have been.

I knew that Michael was an unhappy, tortured individual. I had read long ago that those who torture are tortured themselves. A few times in our lives I had caught a glimpse of the kind of man Mike could have been, and the loss of that man was agony for me. It was to this man that I wrote this letter before going into surgery. I found it among his things after he was gone:

Dear Michael,

I pray that the spirit of the man who cried with joy with me at the birth of our children, and grieved with me over the loss of our little one will be the spirit that reads this letter.

I do not want to add to your life, at this time, any recriminations or blame. I only wish I could convey to you what you have meant to me, and what you mean to me still.

Our life together has either been heaven or hell, love or hate, joy or deepest pain. Now that we seem to have come to the end of our journey together, I know that each of us has deep regrets for what might have been.

I have mingled my tears with you over our Kathy and Donnie, joined you in laughter, and fought the anger that has lived with you since you were a child.

My prayer now is that even though our marriage seems to be at an end that the many wonderful things we have shared will enable us to part as friends.

This surgery that I'm to have this Wednesday would be extremely hard for me under the best of circumstances, because I'm so frightened to get on that operating table once again. Yet, my fright is nothing compared to the loss of your love and support behind me, when I go through this particular valley. I ask you, not because of your feeling for me now, but because of what you have felt, to pray for me and wish me well.

Mike, our children are going through a very traumatic time right now. I know that you feel from their attitude that they don't care. Believe me this is not the case. They are just so unsure of how to handle themselves, so awkward in a situation they have no control over, so embarrassed by emotions that they know not only they are feeling, but we are feeling too, that they have compromised by not saying anything.

Their security is falling down around their ears. There is no way we or they can escape this fact. John is especially susceptible because he has never been sure of your love. You are his dad, and the role he expected you to play in his life is not being played.

At his age the butterfly is expected to leave the cocoon, but the cocoon is expected to stay solid and steady for him to return to. To some extent I identify with his feelings because you have also been my father as well as my husband, and I too, have always expected you to be here.

Now, without wanting to sound maudlin, I want to come to the reason of this letter. I simply can't go into surgery without saying or at least writing these words.

Mike, with all my heart I ask you to forgive me for the times I must have failed you. I had a problem from the very beginning. You were much too complex for me at seventeen and I never seemed able to grow into the job. It was not that you were not loved, I was just not adequate.

Forgive me,
Betty

I sincerely meant these words because no one can come to the end of a relationship of so many years without many regrets over what might have been. I could not help wondering if I had been stronger, the kind of person who would never have given in to Mike's nonsense, maybe he would have straightened out his life.

I remember asking him this question one time, "Mike, if you had known, without a shadow of a doubt, that I would have left you if you fooled around, would you have done it?" His instant reply was, "No." I will never know whether this would have been the case, but I wish I had never asked the question.

CHAPTER 16

Laurie, My Forgiving Child

Mike's total indifference during my stay in the hospital really bothered me. I thought that for the children's sake he at least should have stayed closer to home. My housekeeper told me that he hadn't even come home most of the nights I was gone. He should have been home. Laurie, his daughter, needed him desperately and he wasn't even there.

Laurie attended Melodyland High School, and on the day of my surgery she was hurrying home to check with our housekeeper and then come to the hospital. As she drove away from the school, she was flagged down by two young men. She thought she knew them until they reached the car. Then it was too late.

They opened her door, dragged her out, and took her to their nearby car. As they drove away, Laurie was crying and begging them not to hurt her. All her tears were to no avail. She was brutally raped by the two men. When they took her back to her car, she was barely coherent from shock. The warning of the men rang loud and clear in her ears. "Don't you tell anyone what happened. If you do, we know where to come to get you!"

Laurie didn't know what to do. Her father was gone. I was on the operating table. She was also afraid that if I found out Mike couldn't be found, it would be the bitter end for Mike and me.

It is amazing how far children will go to preserve their families, even when they have deteriorated into something like ours had. The specter of divorce is much more frightening to them than the tears, the fights, and the horrible words. At any rate, Laurie decided to keep what had happened from us both.

She had a close friend named Robbie. There was nothing

romantic between them then, they were just special to each other. It was Robbie she turned to. Robbie took care of her like she was his little sister. He went as far as to take her to school the next few weeks, with a gun at his side, in case the men returned.

After I got home from the hospital and recuperated enough that I was aware of something besides how I felt, I realized that something was terribly wrong with Laurie.

Laurie was a beautiful sixteen year old, but lately she hadn't looked good. She looked wan and pale, and was obviously neglecting her makeup and hair. I was used to nagging her to get away from the mirror, before she took root there! Now she hardly glanced at the mirror.

I was used to the girl who wouldn't go to the store for a loaf of bread until she looked, as her brother put it, "snappy." Now it appeared like she wanted to look plain. She was wearing no makeup at all and her hair looked drab and lifeless.

Another problem also was cropping up. She wouldn't go to school. Every excuse she could think of, she gave. The days she would go to school, I would find out later she had ditched. Paul and Cindy found out when the principal of the school, knowing how close they were to us, asked them about Laurie's frequent absences.

After Paul and Cindy told me about Laurie's absences at school, they offered to come by on their way to Melodyland to work each morning, pick up Laurie and take her to school, and then return her home after school. That would assure her going to school. It was when I told her of this plan that Laurie went to pieces and finally told me what was wrong.

How can I tell you what it feels like to hear this horrible experience related, not from the lips of some stranger on TV, but from the mouth of your own child? We have all seen the anguished face of some poor woman on the evening news or read in the morning paper of some helpless girl who found herself in the hands of some monster with a perverted mind, but these things happen to other people's daughters, never to ours. Now I had to face the fact that it had happened to my Laurie.

Suddenly, all the pieces of the puzzle fell into place. Laurie wasn't going to school because she was afraid the men would come back and get her, and she had let her appearance go because they had told her they were raping her because no one as pretty as she was should be a virgin. I cried out to Laurie, "Honey, why didn't you tell me! I could have helped you. This is what a mother is for. You didn't give me a chance to comfort you, take you for medical attention, and do all the things I could have done to make it easier."

Laurie's answer to me hurt me nearly as much as the terrible thing that had happened to her. She said, "Mom, I was afraid if you knew, you would leave Daddy, and I didn't want to be responsible."

She didn't want to be responsible. We had made such a terrible botch of our lives, and she didn't want to be responsible. Bless her heart, she had read me right. If I had known at the time this happened, that her father was not at the hospital, and not available to his kids in case of emergency, I would have left so fast he wouldn't have seen me going!

Well, it was high time for me to come through for her now, so I promised I wouldn't say anything to her father. I got her to a doctor as quickly as possible. The doctor said there was some scar tissue on her cervix, but he thought she would be all right.

That night I held my little girl in my arms and cried the tears that should have been wept weeks ago. I was crying not only for the pain she had experienced. I was crying because I hadn't managed to give her the home she deserved. I loved my children more than anything and I hadn't given them a home where they could feel secure.

I talked it over with Laurie and I decided to let her quit high school and finish her subjects at home. Arrangements were made for this, and she enrolled in a beauty college to take cosmetology.

A few weeks after she had settled into her new routine we were having a mother-daughter talk, late one night. I really felt I was talking to a young woman, not my little girl anymore. This experience had matured her overnight. Laurie said, "Mom, the Lord has let me know that if I will forgive the men for what they did to me, he will erase it from my mind."

I said, "Honey, do you think it is possible for you to do this?" Her unhesitating "Yes!" was enough for me to say, "Well, let's get on our knees and pray about it."

So, in my bedroom, kneeling with my arms around her, my daughter gave this terrible thing to the Lord. She told him that she forgave the men, and asked Jesus to save them.

There are times in your life when something happens that justifies all the hell you go through, all the sacrifice you make. In my Laurie I at last had a success by the grace of God. She is the daughter all mothers desire and a Christian who puts the rest of us to shame.

When I had Dr. Pickering talk to Laurie a few months later, he told me that he had never seen such a remarkable recovery from such a devastating experience. he said it was like it had never happended to her. This is what Jesus had promised her.

What a difference it makes when you have Jesus to turn to when the world hands you an experience so horrible that it could warp you for the rest of your life! Unfortunately, many women, even though they are Christians, undergo rape and are unable to give their problems to the Lord. Over the years I have counseled with troubled women who have been raped. They often allow this terrible experience to, in effect, "rape" them daily for the rest of their lives.

It might help if these women could understand that rape is not really a sex crime. Rather, it is an assault by someone who is so mad at the world that he has to take it out on someone else.

Many cities have recognized the need for good counseling for rape victims. Most metropolitan areas have special rape crisis centers where rape victims can receive positive help. A quick call to your telephone operator can connect you with caring people who want to help.

CHAPTER 17

Closing The Door
For The Last Time

One of the main reasons Laurie didn't want me to tell her father about what had happened was that she didn't want to do anything that might jeopardize the help he was seeking. When I got out of the hospital, I told Mike I was going to get a divorce if he didn't get some help. He must have thought I meant it, because he agreed to go to see Dr. Pickering.

He kept insisting that I go to his sessions with him. He said he didn't have anything to hide. I didn't want to go with him, because I knew from my own experience that you need to be able to say anything you please to the doctor, without worrying what someone else is thinking. The doctor said it was all right for me to be there for a few sessions, but he hoped Mike would agree to go "solo" after a while.

It soon became obvious what Mike was up to. The sessions turned into recitations of Mike's innocence. When Dr. Pickering would ask him why he was away from home so much, Mike would explain that he was redoing all his master teaching tapes at a lab in the valley, forty miles away. He said they let him use the facility at night, and it was a marvelous opportunity to correct and edit his tapes. Of course, there were hundreds and hundreds of tapes, so this project was going to take a long time.

When the doctor would ask him why his family could only reach him by his answering service, he would answer, "I've so many commitments, between my teaching, my counseling, my speaking engagements, and taping that I felt this way they could always find me." As Alyson Fry used to say, "No one could look as wide-eyed and innocent, while they were totally guilty, as Mike Esses."

If Dr. Pickering brought up the other women in his life, Mike would jump in with assurances that they were all in the past, and his love for me was stronger than ever. The doctor would say, "But Mike, your wife doesn't feel that this is the case." Mike replied that I was paranoid because of what had happened in the past, and I had to learn to forgive.

Mike didn't fool Dr. Pickering. He knew that Mike was only seeing him to appease me. He just didn't know why.

Well, I knew why. Dr. Pickering was not from a fundamental or charismatic background, and didn't understand that the stringent, no divorce, ethic that predominates that movement was rigidly enforced, especially against the clergy. It was nearly occupational suicide for a minister to get a divorce, and Mike knew it.

One weekend I had a couple of speaking engagements around San Diego, so I left on Friday to go to Temecula, which is about halfway to San Diego, for an afternoon Women Aglow meeting.

I told my housekeeper that I would be back Sunday, because I planned to see the Robleys on Saturday, and then come home Sunday after my speaking engagement. I hadn't been able to tell Mike of my plans because I hadn't seen him for several days.

Sitting at the speaker's table at the Friday afternoon luncheon, I looked out over the room filled with chattering ladies, excited over the meeting, waiting to hear this woman speak on family life and how to save your marriage, and I knew I couldn't continue this nightmare much longer. I didn't want to try to help them, I wanted them to help me. I was the one who was sinking.

After the meeting, I sat in my car for awhile, just trying to pull myself together. A thought occured to me. I have the time this evening, why don't I call Walter Martin and ask if I can come to talk with him? I knew he lived nearby. Maybe he wouldn't be busy. When I called Walter, he was very pleasant, and told me I was welcome to come. In fact, he asked me to stay and have dinner with his family.

When I arrived at his home, Walter and I went to his study and I asked him the question that was so important. I asked him if I had biblical grounds to obtain a divorce. Walter said, "Before I answer, I want you to tell me what's going on. Every time I ask

Mike if everything is all right with you two, he always assures me you couldn't be happier. He has told Ralph the same thing and now you're here talking about divorce!"

I said, "Walter, things are not all right. In fact, they couldn't be worse. If you're going to talk to Mike about his marriage, you have to have me there to keep him from lying."

Walter said, "OK, that's what we will do. I'll set up a meeting right now." Walter reached for the phone and called Melodyland and got Paul Roper on the phone. He told Paul he wanted to set up a meeting with Pastor, Paul, Mike, Betty, and himself, to try to deal with the Esses' marriage.

The incredulous look that appeared on Walter's face as he listened to Paul's reply piqued my curiosity. Walter finally said, "Just a minute, Paul," and turned to me and said, "Paul says there is a problem about a meeting. It seems Mike just called from Palm Springs and he is totally hysterical because he says he has found you in a motel with the man you were involved with last year."

Walter turned back to the phone, and said, "Paul, Betty is sitting right here in front of me. Mike is lying." Paul must have been shocked. At any rate, the men set up a conference call between Paul and Ralph in Anaheim, Mike in Palm Springs, and Walter in San Juan Capistrano. Walter had me get on his extension.

When the call was established, Mike immediately began to yell, "I've found her. I've got her dead to rights! She's here in a motel with that man, and I'm going to confront her and bring you men back proof of her adultery!"

Ralph kept trying to interrupt him, and finally Mike let him get a word in. Ralph said, "Mike, you're trying to set your own wife up." With that, Mike went on another tirade about how loyal he had always been to Ralph, how he had never lied to him, and now Ralph was accusing him, instead of helping him. Finally Ralph said, "Betty, why don't you say something?"

It was hard for me to say anything. I was crying with embarrassment and betrayal, and I wished I would never have to face these men again. Finally I said, "Mike, I'm here at Walter's, and I can account for my whole day."

Walter took over then: "Mike, we will see you tomorrow at the Grand Hotel, across from Melodyland. We will take a room for this meeting. Be there."

After Walter hung up the phone, I sat there in a state of complete shock. I felt disbelief, betrayal, shame, bewilderment, and, finally, overwhelming fury. I was so angry at Mike's treachery, that I blurted out the one secret Mike would have done anything to keep from Walter: "Mike's a complete phony, Walter! He even made up his rabbinical ordination!"

It was now Walter's turn to be furious. Mike had manipulat -ed Walter into putting his reputation on the line for a phony.

I lay in bed that night, stunned with the enormity of what Mike was willing to do to me. I thought, "Dear God, what could have happened to me if I had gone ahead and checked into a motel and seen a movie by myself, like I had planned? He would have had me, and I probably never would have been able to establish my innocence. Who in the world would think the man was capable of doing something this terrible to his wife?"

The next day Michael was waiting for us when we pulled into the parking lot. He started yelling and screaming and Walter told him to shut up until we got up to the room. Walter was disgusted with him not only because of his phony ordination, but also because Mike had called at midnight the night before to read off a list of men I was supposed to have had affairs with. Some of the names I knew, others I never even heard of.

When all of us got to the room, it proved to be quite a session. Mike was totally out of control, and was using every four letter word in the book. He was cornered and he knew it. He began making threats about how he was going to take care of me, and how I was an adulteress. Walter told him that I had repented for my adultery, and I was as clean as if it never happened, because I had truely repented. He told Mike that he didn't want to hear another word about it. In fact, he said, "If I hear that you are maligning this woman anymore, I'm going to use all the influence I have coast to coast to stop you." Then Walter started in on Mike in earnest. He nailed him about his fraudulent rabbinical papers. "How dare you use my name to cover up your rotten scheme!"

Mike tried to stammer out an apology — he knew he was exposed now. With that Mike simmered down, and said he was leaving. Before he left he turned to Pastor Wilkerson and said, "Ralph, if I go down, you're going to go with me!"

Mike's words shocked Ralph. He knew what Mike meant. He knew that if he didn't salvage this situation for Mike somehow, he could count on Mike to spread the word about his own one indiscretion. This was the sword over Pastor's head over and over again, not only with Mike, but with anyone who found out his secret.

His problem was Allene. She probably could forgive any sin in the world except infidelity. He honestly felt he was finished if she found out what he had done.

We all sat stunned as Mike walked out the door. Walter turned to Ralph and said, "Ralph, if we don't do something about this, God is going to hold us responsible." Before they left the room, they decided to have a meeting at Walter's, with Dr. Pickering included. They decided that they needed his input to decide what should be done, because Mike definitely appeared to be unbalanced.

The meeting was held and Pickering told them that Mike needed help, but he wasn't sick enough to force him to get it, and he didn't think he would get it on his own. Paul suggested that he be given a month off to be by himself and see if he couldn't pull himself together. Dr. Pickering said that he didn't think it would help, but it was up to them. The men turned to me and asked if I would hold off taking any divorce action for a month. I agreed.

This was an interesting month. There was peace, because I knew that Mike wouldn't pop in at any time. I wanted things to work out, so I spent hours every day in prayer. I was closer to the Lord than ever before. The children were comfortable because there was no bickering and fighting. On the whole, it was a little like the soldiers' R and R (rest and relaxation).

Finally, it was time for Michael to come back. He had been gone a month. He was supposed to go to Mexico, just rest on the beach, and try to come to terms with God. I hadn't heard a word from him the entire time he was gone, so I had no idea what progress had been made. I was to learn shortly.

One evening I received a phone call from him. He told me that he would be in the following night, but he would just be passing through to pick up some clean clothes for a meeting he had in another city.

I asked him how he was, and what he had been doing, but he interrupted me with a few cuss words about my nosiness. When I said "Mike, don't use that language with me," he said, "Well, how about if I tell you to go _____ yourself." I just looked at the phone for a moment and without another word, I hung up.

To say I was mad wouldn't even approach how I felt. To say I was furious was a little closer, but it still isn't strong enough. I was so outraged, I was nearly out of my mind. How dare he use that word on me, after I had spent a month in prayer that God would touch him! The next morning I saw my attorney, and when Mike came by for his clothes that night, he was also served with divorce papers.

It didn't take Mike long to swing into action, to try to get me to drop the divorce. Everyone we knew was soon knocking on my door, pleading Mike's cause. He kept my phone ringing day and night, begging me just to see him and talk this over. As far as I was concerned, there wasn't anything to talk about, so I kept hanging up on him.

A few weeks later our accountant, Bill Dumas, called and told me that I had to come in about some taxes. I asked him if Mike would be there, and Bill said, yes, it was necessary, that we would be in trouble with the government if this matter wasn't straightened out. I couldn't imagine why I was needed, as Mike had never let me know anything about our financial business. I never even saw my own checks. As soon as I would come home from speaking engagements with checks, or my royalty checks would come in the mail, Mike would take them, have me endorse them, and I never saw them again.

Anyway, I agreed to go to the office, and when I arrived Mike was already there. It was apparent from the beginning that the tax matter was only a ruse to get me to talk to Mike, with Bill functioning as an intermediary.

I figured, if this is what Mike wants, this is what he is going to get. I told them that I would only talk if I could have my say first, without any interruption. They agreed and I exploded. Everything I ever wanted to say to Mike Esses, I said. For the first time, I spoke straight from my heart, unloading the hurt of years of forced compromise and punishment for Mike's sins. After more than fifteen minutes, I was finished. I stopped.

Mike sat there for a moment, then he turned to Bill: "Everything the woman said was true." He even admitted that he had been living with another woman during his month of "prayer." He also said, "These last few weeks have been hell for me, because I realized what I lost."

That sounded good, but I wasn't buying. I had been through too much and I didn't want any more. I got up to leave, and Bill stopped me. He asked me, as a personal favor to him, to talk with a minister neither Mike nor I knew, and let him counsel with us.

Reluctantly, I agreed, and Bill drove us over to meet with this man. I could tell right away that this was not going to be an ordinary counseling session. The first words out of the man's mouth were directed to Mike: "Sir, you are a phony." This minister's name was Don West, and he had Mike on the ropes before Mike knew what was happening to him. Mike was blanching whiter and whiter as the man verbally took him apart. He confronted Mike with his adulteries, his lying spirit, his gutter mouth, his manipulating of God's people for financial gain, his theft of God's money. He even told him: "Your wife doesn't know yet, but you have taken your assets and have them hidden outside the country. Besides all of this, you are still involved with your latest affair. Now, you are going to have to make a decision. God is tired of fooling around with you. I must warn you to be very careful about making this decision. If you make the decision to walk with Satan, God will leave you alone, and you can at least have the blessings of Satan for the rest of your life. Then you will go to hell.

"But, if you make the decision to follow God, and you turn from him again, you will spend your remaining days unable to move, until God finally lets you die. Then you will go to hell."

Mike and I looked at each other in shock when the pastor said these words. They were confirmation of a dream Laurie had many months prior to this. Laurie had come to me sobbing one morning, she was so frightened from a dream she had. After she told me what it was, she said, "I have to tell Dad when I see him." The next morning he was home, and a trembling Laurie related to her father what God had showed her. This had never happened to her before and she was scared to death.

She said, "Dad, you were lying in bed and you couldn't move from the neck on down. We were all around you, but you couldn't see us, and you thought you were alone. You kept crying out to God that you were sorry, but he wouldn't believe you. He said you had said this all before, and you didn't mean it. So, now he was going to let you lie there and think about how you treated your family and how you lived your life, then when he felt it was time, he would let you die, and you would go to hell."

Mikes reaction, at the time, was devastating to Laurie. His only comment was, "Well if going to hell will get me away from her (pointing at me) it would be worth it." He then stompted out of the house, leaving a shattered child behind him.

Mike sat for a moment in front of this pastor, remembering, before he answered: "I will answer like Joshua and say, 'Me and my house will serve the Lord.' "

Don West pinned him down even more. He said, "Mike, I'm not talking about your household. I know they serve the Lord. They aren't the problem, you are the problem. What are *you* going to do?"

Mike said, "I am going to serve the Lord." I just prayed that Mike realized the magnitude of that answer.

The pastor now turned to me and said, "Betty, you are going to have to go back to Mike, one more time. If he fails you again, you will be free." I started to cry because I didn't want to go back. I tried to stammer out my objections as he told me in the kindest manner possible that he heard me and he understood, but God was requiring this of me.

I told him that I just couldn't give him my answer yet. I had bookings up north and while I was away, I would pray and seek the Lord. At this point, we left and I drove home. I knew I was stalling for time, because I knew that I had heard from God. This was the most unusual day of my life. I had seen God in action through the supernatural discernment of this pastor. I just needed time to accept it.

When I got back from my engagements, Mike was waiting for me at the airport. He told me that he had talked to Pastor Wilkerson, and Pastor was going to let him speak to the congregation next Sunday. Everybody at Melodyland knew that we were in the process of a divorce, so there was quite a stir when Mike and I and Pastor walked down the aisle that Sunday.

Pastor told the crowd that Mike had something to say to them. Michael grabbed me by the hand and began to speak. He told the audience that he had sinned against God, that he had sinned against his wife,and he had sinned against the congregation by not being the man he should have been. He told them that he had asked forgiveness from me, and I had agreed to give him another chance. "Now," he said, "I'm asking your forgiveness."

Pastor stepped in at that moment and said, "I want to know if you want to give Mike another chance. Mike has agreed to go for professional help for his problems and he says he will put forth every effort to straighten out his life. Do you want him back as your teacher?" The crowd stood as one, giving Mike a standing ovation.

When I went to see my attorney, and told him to drop the divorce suit, he looked at me with compassion and said, "Betty, wait a while before you drop this suit." I explained to him what had happened, and about Mike's public declaration of his intentions and of his earnest agreement to seek professional help.

He said, "That's fine, and I hope for your sake that he is sincere, but with Mike's track record, you need to cover yourself. You don't have to execute the suit, you can just keep it pending. Mike doesn't even have to know, so he can't accuse you of keeping a sword over his head. All I'm asking you to do is protect yourself."

My attorney told me that over the years he had seen many men, taken by surprise by a divorce action, desperately seek a reconciliation for one reason: they try to get back as quickly as possible so they can hide their assets, before the divorce action commences again.

I told him, "Wade, you don't understand. Mike's already done this. He's got $300,000 in Treasury Bills and $150,000 worth of jewelry out of the country already. He admitted this to me. He's got them in a bank down in Mexico."

Wade looked at me like I was crazy: "You've decided to go back to someone who would do this to you and your children?" Sheepishly, I defended my action saying, "Mike's told me that he will bring it all back as soon as possible." Wade just shook his head and said, "OK, Betty, it's your funeral, but the handwriting is on the wall."

I left Wade's office feeling very dejected. I wondered if maybe the man was right and I should have kept the divorce pending. Mike had promised to return our assets, but I certainly had no guarantee. But, I had agreed to give this marriage one more try, and I was going to have to trust the Lord all the way. As I drove home, I tried to dismiss my attorney's warning, and started to concentrate on the positive.

Mike began going back to Dr. Pickering, only now I didn't go with him, except when the doctor requested my presence.

Mike was doing very well at home. He was accounting for his time, even though I never asked. I always knew where he was. Every night saw him home with his family, and I even gave him a big birthday party on April 28th. Many of our friends were there to wish him well and tell him how happy they were that our marriage was on the mend.

There was only one thing still nagging me. Our assets were still down in Mexico. I didn't say much, because I didn't want it to look like money was all I was interested in. When I did ask Mike about it, he would put me off by saying, "As soon as I get time to make the trip down there, I will. In the meantime, everything is safe, so don't you worry about it." The turning point came in June, when we received a phone call from someone on the committee of *Jesus '79.* This was a huge outdoor meeting being held that summer in Northern California. Many well-known evangelists and musicians would be appearing there.

Mike and I were both booked for the meeting, and were looking forward to it. The man on the phone asked for Mike, and informed him that his invitation was cancelled because of his marital problems. I spoke to the man then and he said that they hoped I would still be part of the meeting. I told him that I wouldn't think of participating in their meeting now, and I told him that he and his committee had no business sitting in judgment. After all, the sin was committed against God and Mike had repented and was forgiven.

Later, we tracked down the person who had informed and primed the committee to make this decision. We found out it was a minister at Melodyland who had a running feud with Michael.

With this act this pastor fanned the flames of Michael's destruction. He totally regressed to his former behavior, and the next few months became a nightmare.

Mike's sessions with Dr. Pickering were the first to go. Then the home life he had re-established was totaled. It soon became obvious that he had picked up again with the woman he had been living with before or that he had formed a new alliance. He no longer lived at home.

One day he came by to pick up some clothes, and we had more harsh words. When Mike left that day, I sat in our bedroom and talked to the Lord. I told him that I had done what he had asked of me. I had returned to Mike. I reminded him of his promise that if Mike failed me again, I could leave, and I would never have to return again. I felt that I had kept my end of the bargain and now I was free. Then I went to the phone and called my lawyer.

I saw Michael one time after that. He came by the house and asked me if I had seen my attorney. I said, "Yes, I have. You'll be hearing from him soon." Mike then proceeded to call me every filthy name at his command. I took this verbal assault without a word, because I knew I was hearing these miserable obscenities for the very last time.

As Mike turned from me to stalk out the door, he shouted, "YOU WILL NEVER SEE ME AGAIN!" I stood there and looked into the eyes of the man I had lived with for twenty-eight years. I had given him children and I had loved him with all my heart. Now it was my moment of truth. Slowly I squared my shoulders and with all the dignity I could muster up, I said, "Is that a promise, Mike?" And I closed the door.

It was over. Twenty-eight years of trying to make something work that was probably doomed from the start. I had tried everything I knew to make it succeed. I'd gone down every road, highway, street, avenue, and by-way trying to find the answer to what made Mike tick, and I never found out.

I'll never forget Grace Robley saying to me, "Betty, you keep running on the field with one new play after another, and Mike has already gone home. The lights are off and the stadium is empty. You're playing the game all by yourself." Grace was right. It had been a game of solitaire, all along, and I was just too dumb to realize it.

CHAPTER 18

Rumors

Mike meant what he said as he walked out of our home. It has been almost four years since we have seen him, but we certainly have heard from him, about him, and of him. My attorney served him with more divorce papers on October 3, 1979, while he was at Melodyland. I was told that Mike went berserk when the man handed him the papers. He threw them on the ground, and began cursing and screaming that he didn't want them. The process server just said, "Sir, you have been served." That was the last day Melodyland saw Michael Esses. We all assumed that he had left the country in order to pick up his money in Mexico.

Paul and Cindy came by nearly every evening after work, to cheer me up and talk with my children. They also brought the mail that arrived for Mike and me at Melodyland. One evening they brought the first of many bills that quickly became an avalanche.

It seems that Mike had taken all our credit cards and had gone on a binge of buying, swiftly charging thousands of dollars worth of merchandise. He had opened many new accounts I knew nothing about, and had the bills sent to Melodyland. This was all done during three days in the latter part of October.

Paul, Cindy, and I would open these bills every night, to see what Mike had bought. There was a wide range of things, including diamond rings, watches, all kinds of clothing, fishing tackle, a gun, sheets, pillows, comforters, towels, shocks for his car, etc.

One night as we opened the bills, Cindy gave a gasp of surprise, and was reluctant to hand me the bill she had just opened. As I read it I could see why she was so hesitant. The bill was for baby things, clothing and furniture. Now we knew why Mike had been miserable those last few months. The man was starting his third family while he was still with his second family. He was trapped.

I couldn't keep the tears out of my eyes, and finally I had to leave the room for a minute to pull myself together. I had suspected something like this. In fact, I had asked Mike once if he was in too deep to get out, but this kind of confirmation was hard to take.

This man had been my husband for all those years, and the father of my children. It was hard to imagine him sharing this experience with someone else.

We had known that the woman Mike was involved with was young, about twenty-five to Mike's fifty-seven, but to tell the truth, I thought Mike was too smart to get her pregnant. Now I knew why he had no choice in the matter. Christians may forgive you for sinning, but they have a hard time with stupidity. No one has to get pregnant in this day and age. Certainly Mike was old enough and experienced enough to know better.

Out of curiosity, I called Bullocks and asked the clerk if she could remember Mike and the diamond ring he had bought. She didn't hesitate a minute. She remembered him well. She thought it was so sweet of the minister to buy his wife a diamond wedding band for their anniversary

After I hung up the phone, I thanked God that I was finally free of Mike's bondage. Otherwise I could never have survived this further indignity. He had not only pulled out of here with all of our assets, he had the gall to leave me with the bills to pay for his mistress's wedding ring and their baby's furniture.

California is a community property state and I was just as responsible for his bills as he was for mine. The only difference was, I had run up no bills and he had run up about $20,000 worth.

When Michael left he took everything with him. When I went to the bank, not only the bank account had been stripped, but he had even taken the money in the children's Christmas Club, and Christmas was only a month away. Fortunately, we had just sold some property in Mexico and I would receive that money in a couple of months. In the meantime, Paul loaned me the money to get by on, and I began selling my jewelry.

The next trick he tried was to reverse the sale on the property in Cabo San Lucas, Mexico. The woman who had purchased it called me one day, frantic because the sale wasn't going through. I called my attorney, and he got before a judge who gave me permission to make the sale since it was my part of the community property. Mike apparently had planned on living down in Mexico, and this ruined his plans.

I have a letter from the woman who bought the condominium and she states that she spoke to Michael several times during October and November (on one day almost hourly). He told her that he and his wife were getting a divorce and he was going to go to Israel to live.

Michael called other people at Melodyland and said that he had gone to Mexico for a rest, had a very serious stroke, and had been nursed by a husband and wife who were completed Jews. These are just two of the stories he came up with.

Paul and Cindy sat down with me and figured out my next course of action. The first thing I had to do was get out from under the responsibility of the leased cars for which Mike had contracted. When I told the leasing agents I couldn't possibly pay for these cars, they were very nice. They told me that since it had been Mike who had leased all the cars, they were his responsibility, not mine.

My attorney started writing letters to all the department stores, letting them know the circumstances behind all the charges. Some of them said I would still have to pay Mike's bills, but others said they would not hold me responsible. They said they would file a civil suit for fraud against Mike since he had charged these things without any intention of paying for them.

One thing that helped me with the creditors was that my attorney was able to say that my divorce suit had been pending for nine months. It seems Wade hadn't listened to me and had never dropped my first suit. When I came back to him, he was too much of a gentleman to say, "I told you so." But, he did tell me that because the first suit was still in effect, I would be completely free of Mike in about four months. In the meantime, I tried putting my life together once again.

One person who was a tremendous help was Bob DeBlase. A few weeks after Mike left, Bob called and asked to see me. We met for lunch, and Bob informed me that he had left Marie and had filed for divorce. When I started to protest, Bob stopped me by saying, "Betty, you know this has been coming for a long time. Every pastor we know and most of our friends, including you, have tried to help make this marriage work, but it just doesn't help. The only thing that Marie really wants is everything we've got, so I've given it to her. The house, the furniture, the car, the bank account. The only things I took with me are my clothes, my leased car, and enough money to get an apartment. Everything I've worked for over the last thirty years is gone, but I don't care. I've got my freedom."

I knew that Bob's children were now grown and on their own. In fact, his son was married and had made Bob a grandfather twice, so his children were out of the nest and would not be too adversely affected by their parents' divorce.

After what I had been through, there was nothing in me that could say any longer, "Hang in there, Bob. If you try another thirty years, you might make it work." I just accepted the fact that the failure of their marriage was inevitable.

It seemed, during this same period, many of the people I knew were avoiding me. I didn't realize it for awhile because I was too busy trying to adjust to my new life, but finally I began to wonder if something was wrong.

Then one day Laurie came into the house with her eyes swollen from crying. She didn't want to tell me what was wrong, but I finally coaxed it out of her.

She was at her beauty school, and was working on a customer's hair. The woman recognized the name Esses on Laurie's smock, and she turned around and asked Laurie if her father was Michael Esses. When Laurie said that he was, the woman went into a tirade. In front of everyone in the school, she told Laurie she should be ashamed of who she was. She said that her mother was as bad as her father for covering for him, so that he was able to fool all the people.

Laurie tried to ignore what she was saying, but that seemed to aggravate the woman even more. She began shaking her finger in Laurie's face, and continued telling her how ashamed she should be. Laurie never said one word to the woman. She just turned, walked out the door, and came home.

I thought, this woman probably thinks she is a good Christian, and wouldn't commit the more obvious sins for all the tea in China, but she had just hurt this young girl, who was already suffering from the situation, and she would never even have a twinge of conscience about it.

Because of the woman's reaction to Laurie, I asked one of my friends about what was being said at Melodyland about our situation. She said, "Betty, I have heard so many different stories that they would boggle your mind! There is only one common denominator. Most of the stories have come from Mike." It seems Mike was staying in contact with enough people from the church that he could keep feeding back lies. Of course, there were enough people with vivid imaginations there to fill in the gaps. The stories varied considerably, but the one thing they all had in common was that Mike was aways pictured as grievously ill.

One woman called and said she was so sorry this had happened to us, but it only showed how much Mike loved his family, that he would be willing to go off and die by himself to spare us the agony of his death.

From his niece we heard he was being taken care of by a Jewish couple, who were having to sell their jewelery and were in danger of losing their home because of the expense of caring for Mike. They were so poor that they couldn't afford a telephone, so Mike had to call his niece from a telephone booth, she couldn't call him.

Next the niece was told that the Jewish couple had gone back to Israel, and Mike now had a widow with a young child caring for him. When she asked him for his address so she could come see him, he told her that he looked too bad and didn't want her to see him like that.

She was so concerned for Mike that she sent him money at the post office box address he provided. This was really a cruel thing for Mike to do to his niece. They had been raised together and she loved him dearly.

The next version of Mike's story I heard from Moishe Rosen. I talked to him on the phone one day about what Mike was doing and what he might do. Moishe asked me if I knew what Mike's story was on our breakup. I told Moishe that I had heard so many versions I didn't know what Mike would come up with next.

Moishe said Mike had contacted his publisher about his royalty checks and had told him that he was in this terrible position because of his wife's numerous affairs and her greed for money. Mike said that because of all my affairs he had gone before the board of elders at Melodyland. He told them he couldn't take any more, and he was going to have to sue me for divorce. The elders are supposed to have advised him to go away to fast and pray to see if he couldn't find it in his heart to forgive me.

Mike said that was what he did. He went away and fasted and prayed for forty days, just like Jesus did in the scriptures, and when he had finally determined that he could forgive me, he started to come home. Unfortunately, when he called a friend of his, he was told that I had already divorced him and was seeing another man.

I was seething on the phone, listening to this pack of lies. Finally I said, "Well, Moishe, let me tell you, when he went on that trip for prayer and fasting, I've got the bills to prove that he went well equipped. In fact, he had the makings of a new family with him to keep him company."

That night when Bob came by to take me out to dinner and a movie, I told him I was going to have to get to the bottom of what Mike really did after he left here, in order to put a halt to all these false rumors. I said, "Bob, it's unbelievable what some of these people think. After what Mike did to me, some of them are convinced that I'm the guilty party."

I knew why Michael was doing this. It was necessary for him to be the innocent party for him to have any chance at continuing his ministry, so I knew he was not going to stop telling these stories.

Investigation came up with some of the facts. A few months after they left, Mike had a new baby daughter named Deborah. The mother's name was Billy Jean Davis and she was from New

Mexico, and her father is very active in the Full Gospel Businessmen. She was living with Mike here, because he told our accountant Bill Dumas and me that he was living with a woman here at this time, and we know her child was conceived here in California, while Mike was still married to me.

CHAPTER 19

A New Beginning

My life was beginning to look brighter as each day passed. Bob DeBlase was "courting" me, and it felt so good to be with someone who not only loved me, but also liked and respected me. I had forgotten there was so much to laugh about. I know that Bob felt the same way. Life had been pretty grim for him for a long time. In fact, he confided in me that there were times before when he seriously had contemplated suicide. Now he was happy again.

It was so nice to have fun, and to have someone with whom to enjoy life. Before Mike left, I always felt like a third wheel when I went alone to dinner or to a movie with Paul and Cindy. I knew they invited me because they felt sorry for me, because Mike was never around. Now, when Bob and I went out with them, we were a foursome, and I felt like I belonged.

Paul and Cindy had seen the Esses marriage from very close quarters when we spent two weeks with them in Hawaii one summer. The very first night we were there, problems started. Mike insisted that I unpack everything in his bag, and hang all his clothes up. I didn't want to do this because we were only going to stay one night at this hotel. He became furious with me, so he snapped his suitcase closed, locked it, and said, "Fine, I'll wear the clothes I've got on the rest of the trip," and that's exactly what he did.

He stayed halfway clean by standing in the shower every night, with those same clothes on. He would soap them down, stand with his arms out, rinse them off, then hang them up to dry. Some mornings his clothes weren't dry, but he would just put them on and make do. Paul and Cindy couldn't believe a grown man could act so childish, but to me this was normal behavior for Mike.

In February of 1980, Paul Roper and Henry Block, a financier from Canada, formed a corporation called Church Management Inc. and purchased Melodyland, on a buy-back arrangement, in order to free the church of its debts. Paul had tried to find financing everywhere, but no one would touch Melodyland. Finally, he put himself on the line and produced the financing through CMI.

Paul was involved in so many new projects working with Mr. Block that he couldn't continue giving all his time to Melodyland. So, he set up a management system at the church, and he and Cindy moved to Canada. Bob and I missed them very much. We had grown to love them dearly and to depend on them for their companionship and love.

The relationship between Bob and me was getting quite serious and as the time for his divorce to become final approached, his proposal of marriage sounded tempting. I had come to love him because he was the friend and companion I had always imagined a husband should be. I knew his first concern was for my happiness, not his own. He had shown this when I was divorcing Mike the first time. Bob had called Mike and told him to get back home and take care of his wife and family.

There was one thing I needed to do in order to make a new life for myself. The house was still full of Mike's things. I still hadn't emptied his closet or his chest of drawers in the bedroom. The day my divorce was final, I called a local ministry and told them to come over, that I had a bonanza to give to them. The minister couldn't believe one man had such an extravagent wardrobe.

Mike's closet was jammed with clothes that were scarcely worn, some never worn at all. I began pulling these things out and finally donated forty-one suits (each worth between three and five hundred dollars), a beautiful custom made tuxedo that had never been worn, four sweaters and twenty-nine pairs of shoes (each worth between seventy-five and one hundred dollars). There were twelve belts, twelve pairs of slacks, one hundred and forty-five shirts (some still packaged), three pairs of pajamas, fifteen pairs of walking shorts, twenty-eight pairs of underwear, thirty-seven pairs of socks, and one hundred and fifty-two ties, none of them worth less than twenty dollars. This list shows you the amount of money Mike could afford to spend on clothes and then not even bother to take these things when he left.

One person who benefited from all these clothes was the minister that I called to come get them. He kept saying, "Lord, I only asked you for one new suit, and you've opened the windows of heaven!" I knew he was just getting started in the ministry and he was about Mike's size. This man's delight in all his new clothes shows you that God can take one man's folly and turn it in to another man's blessing. When I had all of Mike's things out of the house, I was able to focus in on Bob with a much better attitude. I guess as long as Mike's things were there I had a nagging worry that he might try to return and spoil everthing.

Bob DeBlase was fast becoming a most important part of my life. The only one of the children who had reservations was John. My son had been through so much with Mike, and he had seen the pain that I had been subjected to by Mike. He didn't want any other man around to cause his family any agony. It was not just Bob, it was any man. I understood what he was going through, and I understood his need to protect me, but I also knew that I couldn't let John's fears control my life.

It was a slow process, but eventually John got more used to the idea that there was every chance that Bob was going to become a permanent part of my life. It gave my great joy later when Laurie told me one day that John told her he was glad I had married Bob.

Remarriage was a scary thing to consider, but Bob's courtship had been laced with flowers and love, laughter and love, and kindness and love. The day came when I couldn't imagine life without him. In fact, a life with him had become the desire of my heart. So, the next time Bob talked to me about marriage, I told him I would love to be his wife.

We called Rob and Grace Robley and asked them if they would perform the ceremony. Their happiness and eagerness to be a part of our marriage was a blessing to both Bob and me, for we had loved and respected these people for years.

The day of our wedding was a beautiful spring day.We all drove down to San Diego where the ceremony was to be held in the Robley's home. It was wonderful to have all my family with me that day, to wish me well. Bob's father was ill, so his parents were unable to come, but Bob's sister Dottie was with us, and we promised to tape the ceremony for his dad and mother.

Rob and Grace had flowers grouped around a beautiful setting in front of their fireplace for our ceremony. As Bob and I stood before them to take our vows, the words of the song we had selected to bless our wedding washed softly over us all.

The song told of two people who were alone and devastated by life, people whose eyes had held tears much too often, and whose lives had been stripped of feelings of worth and love. Now, because they were together, strength and truth, dignity and love, had been restored. Once again, hope for tomorrow was part of their lives.

These words were so appropriate, because this is exactly how Bob and I felt. We knew when we said, "I do," it would be with total commitment to love and honor, cherish and adore, and put the needs of the other before our own. We were not only promising to be husband and wife for life, we were promising to be the best of friends for life. This is what our marriage is based on, and we haven't detoured from this ideal to this day.

A lovely bonus that came with my new marriage is my in-laws, Albert and Margaret DeBlase. One of my most cherished moments came a couple of years after we were married. Margaret made me so happy when she told me for the first time that she loved me. I knew how hard it was for her to express her feelings and so even though I already knew she loved me, her words were precious. Albert and Margaret are both special to me. They are not only my in-laws, they are my close friends.

I had always heard that weddings are catching. Maybe it's the happiness of the newlyweds that inspires the epidemic. Whatever the cause, Bob and I found that the marriage bug had bitten again, right here at home.

A few months after our wedding, I was in a tizzy planning for Laurie's marriage. Her relationship with Robbie had blossomed into love, and both Bob and I were not surprised when they asked our permission to get married. We would have preferred it if they had waited a couple of years, but we knew they were two kids with level heads on their shoulders, so the decision to let them go ahead was made. Laurie was seventeen, going on forty, and Robbie was much the same, as a result of having a lot of adult responsibilities in his home from a very early age.

The day of Laurie's wedding dawned beautiful and clear. Our home had been turned into a wedding chapel with flowers gracing every corner. Bob had removed all of the furniture from our largest room, and the vaulted ceiling added to the wedding atmosphere.

We had rented chairs and they were lined up, row after row, with satin ribbons at the end. Bob had placed a podium and kneeling bench at the head of the room, and they were surrounded by roses from our garden.

This was a wonderful day for Laurie, and I wanted to make it as special as possible for her. I knew that I couldn't replace the one person who was missing and who could make her day complete, but I tried to do the best I could. After Laurie was dressed in her gown, and the flowers were nestled in her hair, I took her aside, away from all her excited attendents and the photographer who was busy snapping pictures of everything in sight.

When I had her alone, I told her I knew how much she missed her father this day, so I wanted her to have the lovely string of pearls and little pearl and diamond earrings her father had given me many years before.

Laurie's pretty face beamed and her eyes began to glisten with tears as she took the pearls from me and put them on with shaking hands. When she turned from the mirror, she gave me a trembling smile and said, "Now I'll be able to feel that Dad has been a part of my wedding."

All her life, Mike had told Laurie he would perform the ceremony on her wedding day. He told her that he would walk her down the aisle first, and then he would go to the podium and perform the wedding ceremony. We used to kid him, because Laurie had always been so special to him, that all this would be hard to do while he was on the floor, kicking and screaming that he wouldn't let her go. Well, he wasn't kicking and screaming today. In fact, we didn't even have the slightest idea where he was.

Laurie looked absolutely beautiful on her brother's arm, coming down the aisle. It was very obvious that John was having a terrible time holding back the tears. I started praying that he would get her to Robbie before he broke down completely.

Then I glanced up at my husband, and he was in the same condition John was in. His problem was a little worse because he had to perform the ceremony. Bob was ordained many years ago, but had never pursued a ministry because he was happy in his career as a consulting engineer. At this moment, from the look on his face, I knew he would much rather be at the office, working out some problem, than standing in front of all of those people, trying his best to keep from crying.

Laurie is special to Bob. He had grown to love her very much. When she asked him to perform the ceremony, he was honored and touched. I just hoped he would be able to make it now. Several times during the ceremony he had to stop for a moment before he could continue. I thought that Rob Robley, who was assisting him, would have to take over finally, but somehow, Bob managed to get to the place where he declared them husband and wife. That was it: my baby was a married woman.

It was only after the ceremony that I realized I hadn't cried at the wedding. Betty Lee, who couldn't smell orange blossoms without welling up, had gone through her own daughter's wedding without shedding a tear. I'm a person who cries at the opening of a supermarket, yet I was dry-eyed and my daughter was the bride. I realized then how tense I had been over John and Bob breaking down. I was so busy praying that God would get *them* through intact, that in the process he got me through with flying colors.

Life began to get back to normal after the wedding. Our furniture was back in our room. The newlyweds were established in the apartment we had fixed for them upstairs. We had two huge rooms and a bath at one end of the house, above the garage, so Bob put an outside door in the garage, and Laurie and Robbie could come and go without us even knowing they were there.

Kathy was happy in her new school, and John had moved in

with a friend into his first apartment. He had a good job as a lead mechanic, and he was savoring his new-found independence.

Bob and I were doing fine together. We were having to watch our budget very carefully because we were paying off many of the bills Mike had charged. Bob wanted to get them out of the way as quickly as possible so that we could forget the past and concentrate on the future.

CHAPTER 20

Christian Coverups

The first bill we got behind us was for $8,000 Mike had borrowed from Melodyland. This was Mike's obligation, but I couldn't stand owing money to the church. As soon as we got this out of the way, we began to pay on all the charge accounts. Slowly but surely we were beginning to make progress. The pile of bills that arrived at the first of each month was beginning to dwindle, and we were beginning to see daylight ahead.

Then, out of the blue, we got a call from my new attorney, Peter Rosen. I couldn't believe what he said to me! Mike had petitioned the court to have my divorce set aside on the grounds that he had no idea I was getting a divorce. He also wanted the property settlement re-evaluated.

I started yelling, "What does he mean, he didn't know I was getting a divorce?! He was served with the papers before he left!" My attorney tried to quiet me down, but he wasn't having much luck. Fortunately, Bob walked into the house at that moment. He had come home for lunch, and he didn't need a crystal ball to tell I was upset. My tears were flowing. Quickly, he took the phone and talked to Peter.

Peter told Bob what he had told me, but was able to add, "Don't worry about this, I'll get a hold of a judge and see what I can do to straighten out this mess."

When Peter called us back, he said, "I've got good news, and I've got bad news. The good news is, the judge would not set your divorce aside, especially since you have remarried. The bad news is, he is going to let Mike have his day in court as far as the property settlement is concerned."

I couldn't begin to understand what Mike thought he was doing. He had gotten much more than his share in the first place.

Attorney's fees were going to have to be paid all over again. It didn't take me long to find out why Mike didn't have to take this fact into consideration.

Mike give his power of attorney to Allen Porterfield, the minister who had ordained him, and Allen and his congregation were paying Mike's attorney fees. Mike had told Allen he didn't have any money.

I called Allen and filled him in about everything Mike had done. But what I said didn't make any difference, because Allen said he was going to help Mike all he could. The only thing he promised was that he would be fair to both of us.

I had a hard time accepting that Allen was being fair to both of us, when because of him, Mike was being financed in this latest scheme with Christians' money, while I was paying my own bills and was still paying on the bills Mike had left behind.

The one thing Allen didn't expect, and Mike didn't consider, was the Pandora's Box Mike was opening with this action. Because of Mike's suit, my attorney and I really started digging into Mike's past and into his financial manipulations. What we found was hard to believe. Mike never should have opened things up again. After we received copies of Mike's depositions from Mike's attorney, we started answering each charge.

In the first place, his allegation that he didn't know he was being divorced was completely refuted by the people at Melodyland who had witnessed the service of the papers, and Mike's ensuing fit. We also had the letter from Mrs. Kasden, the woman who had talked to Mike almost daily after he left Anaheim, about the property in Mexico. Mike had told her repeatedly that he was getting a divorce.

He accused me of claiming that my children were minors, when they weren't. The ages of my children, including their birthdates, were stated quite clearly in my divorce action. What he objected to was that Kathleen was listed as a twenty year old who had only a three year old developmental age. For this reason, my attorney had asked for financial help from her father. I had to care for her for the rest of her life. I then told my attorney to drop this demand since I didn't want anything more from Mike for Kathleen.

Mike stated that he had two $100,000 Treasury Bill Notes, but he failed to reveal that there was an additional $100,000 note he purchased in 1975 and concealed from me. He had told our accountant that he bought it with ministry money and an $11,000 loan from the Bank of America.

I could go on answering each of Mike's allegations with documented proof of their falsity, but what we found out about Mike's financial dealings is much more interesting.

The first big discovery was set up by Mike himself. One day his attorney sent me a list of Mike's personal effects that he had left behind. He was now asking that these things be returned to him.

There was a list of thirty-one items. Some were as big as his library and his wardrobe and some were as ridiculous as requesting half of our sea shell collection and half of our twenty-fifth wedding anniversary presents. I complied with Mike's attorney and sent back twenty-six of the items requested. I couldn't send him his wardrobe since it was long gone, but I did send him a sack of shells and a silver plaque that read, "Happy 25th Anniversary, Mike and Betty Esses." I don't know where he planned to hang it. All in all, I packed up seventy-five cartons for Allen Porterfield to pick up.

Mike's library was the biggest chore of all to sort and pack. My own books were mingled with Mike's, so I had to go through them one by one to determine to whom they belonged before they could be packed.

One set of Mike's books was a huge set of Hebrew encyclopedias. One by one I packed these huge books in the carton. In the process, I uncovered a blue ledger that had been placed behind these heavy books. The notebook obviously had been hidden and when I opened it and read it, I realized why.

It was a detailed ledger of money Mike had received in 1978. Each contributor's name was listed along with the amount he or she had contributed to Mike. There was also a list of some of the honorariums he had received. All of this was entered in Michael's own handwriting. When I totaled the amount of money listed, it came to $150,106. None of this money had ever appeared in our checking account, so I could only assume that Mike had put it in his safety deposit box.

The irony of this discovery is that Mike was shrewd about where he had hidden the ledger. I wouldn't have disturbed those books in a million years, if Mike had not requested them returned.

This same irony applies to the bank book I found while searching through Mike's desk for other items on his list. This book was from the Union Bank and recorded a total of $50,113 in deposits for 1977. I was also totally unaware of where all this money had come from or gone.

Because of the amount of money involved, my attorney decided to subpoena Mike's safety deposit record at Bank of America. More pieces of Mike's financial maneuverings were exposed when this subpoena was answered.

Mike had a total of six different boxes (E-9871, H-2856, C-5699, H-7312, G-7312, and C-5706). All the contents from all of the boxes were removed on July 21, 1978, and all the boxes were closed.

This was during the period that culminated in Mike's sabbatical to Mexico for a month. After he returned, Mike confessed to Bill Dumas, Paul and Cindy Roper, and me that he had taken the contents of those boxes, cash, jewelry, and the Treasury bonds to Mexico and deposited them in a bank there. He never returned these things to this country, to my knowledge.

The bank records also showed that he opened another box (A-9122) on November 7, 1978, which he closed on October 5, 1979. This was one day after I had served him with divorce papers the second time.

Now I had a much clearer picture of Mike's finances. The only money I didn't think I could trace was the money collected in 1979. It was probably in the box Mike closed on October 5, of 1979.

I talked to two different people at Bank of America after the subpoena was served. I asked them what they had observed in Mike's safety deposit boxes. One of them was a loan officer at the bank. She told me that Mike had shown her a box full of cash and gold one time when he was negotiating for a loan.

The person in charge of the boxes told me that Mike would come in with a pile of checks, head straight for the special deposit department, cash the checks, and come immediately to her department. She said she knew this is what he did because he didn't bother taking his box to the private cubicles, he would just have her open the box and he would shove the cash in right in front of her. In fact, she said that Mike was the talk of the bank because everyone knew he was from Melodyland.

All of these things didn't add up to a very pretty picture. There was a lot of money involved that couldn't or hadn't been accounted for. The biggest puzzle of all was why Mike had been screaming poverty ever since he left me.

After my attorney and I put together all the documentation we had gathered on the amount of money Mike left the country with, it proved to be a sizable amount:

$200,000 in Treasury Bill notes, documented by Mike in his deposition to his attorney.

$100,000 in another Treasury Bill revealed to Mike's accountant by Mike himself.

$150,106 documented in Mike's own handwriting in the ledger marked "Contributions for 1978."

$150,000 in jewelry, documented by Mike in his divorce deposition.

$50,113 deposited in Union Bank, documented by the bankbook I found.

$7,000 for his Chevrolet Caprice car, documented by the bill of sale.

The total amount reached $657,219!

If Mike had not opened this case again, I would never have found all this evidence. I was going on with my life, and I had no reason to dig into the past. Now Mike will have to answer to the IRS about where all this money came from and where it went.

Needless to say, when my attorney presented Mike's attorney with all this evidence, Allen Porterfield, who held Mike's power of attorney, was advised to sign the papers and forget about trying to get more money out of me.

My attorney told me that, as a result of all the documentation we had turned up on Michael's holdings, I could sue him for a great deal of money, because I hadn't begun to get my equal share of our community property. I told him that I was content with what I had, because it was legitimately mine. A letter from our accountant, Bill Dumas, was submitted to my attorney after Michael reopened this case. The letter clarifies that I was always kept in the dark about Michael's financial life. (A copy of that letter appears in the appendix.)

CHAPTER 21

Christian Accountability

Laurie and Robbie blessed us with a beautiful granddaughter a little over two years ago. Danielle is the delight of all our lives. Bob is her willing slave, and her "Pa-ka," as she calls him. He is her haven when she is in trouble, her playmate when she can't sit still, and her co-conspirator in her constant search for cookies.

Danielle's future is very important to me. I want the best for her, as all grandparents want for their children. I'm not talking about the material things of life. I have had these things, and I know how meaningless they are without truth and love.

I want her to learn to value what is good, and be able to discard what is bad. I want her to be able to worship in a house of God that is based on the love of Jesus, not the love of fame, notoriety, and popularity.

I want her life as a Christian to be blessed by seeing that service to others who are less fortunate is the prime motivation of the pastors she chooses to have as shepherds of her life.

I don't want her to be satisfied with elaborate churches, grand choirs, and beautifully dressed preachers who have long ago forgotten their humble beginnings. No, I want her to search for humility, kindness, honesty, truth, and not to settle for anything less. If we are not taught by our shepherds' examples that truth is better than a lie; morality is better than promiscuity; honesty is better than deceit; and humility is better than arrogance, then our shepherd has failed miserably in his job.

But, we as God's people also have an obligation in this matter. We need the highest caliber of men to be our leaders. We must recognize, of course, that none of us are perfect, but there should be virtue, decency, and high ethical standards at the core of the men we choose to shepherd us.

I have heard Christians make the observation that they don't care what their minister has done, they still want him for their pastor. That attitude is not going to clean up the church to be without spot or wrinkle, ready for the Lord's return. Where is our responsibility to new Christians, the baby lambs who are just coming in? If we do not provide a place for them that is based on decency and honor, then many of these lambs will fall away because of disillusionment and feelings of betrayal.

Our faith is based on the greatest love God could give his people, the sacrifice of his son. This sacrifice deserves our unwavering dedication in making our Christian world a sanctuary in a world gone mad with man's inhumanity to man, the threat of atomic wipe-out, and the proliferation of every cult known to man. We can't allow that sanctuary to be held up to ridicule in the secular world because of the church corruption we fail to eradicate.

Danielle's birth has made a crusader out of me. All I need is a soap box to stand on, and I start yelling for all Christians to unite to cleanse our world of the rampant impurities that invade our Christian lives. I realize this is an uncomfortable stance to take, but it is our Christian obligation to the Lord to clean his house before the heathen do, whether we like it or not.

Our delight with Danielle made it hard to understand Mike when we found out he had been in Anaheim for over two weeks and never asked to see her. He had stayed with Allen Porterfield's family and we hadn't even known he was in the state. I just couldn't understand Allen. He had been given concrete evidence of Mike's lifestyle and of what he had done to his family. Yet, he continued to promote Mike.

Allen apparently set up several meetings for Mike while Mike was in California. One of my friends attended one of these meetings and was terribly upset by what she heard. Mike stood up and repented for how he had lived his life. He said he had several affairs during our marriage, and he confessed that he had been involved with his present wife while still married to me. He was quite repentant for all these things and asked God to forgive him. Now he was asking the people to forgive him, too. All of this

was well and good, until he added a post script. He just happened to slip in the "fact" that I was guilty of thirty-six affairs during
our marriage. To give this "fact" credence, he added that my
secretary, Betsy Berg, had proof of all these affairs. (A signed
disavowal by Betsy of this accusation is in my possession.)

Only Mike could take my one short affair and expand it to
thirty- six. I couldn't say which emotion was stronger: my horror
at the lie Mike had told, or my disgust with Allen because he had
given Mike a platform to tell it from. Remember, Allen had seen
all the evidence that had been presented to Mike's attorney, and
that evidence would be damning in anyone's sight.

I was even more disappointed a few days later, when a friend
passed along the following letter Allen mailed to over 500 people:

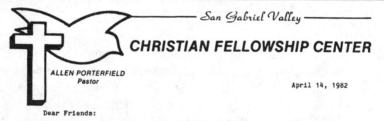

San Gabriel Valley —————

CHRISTIAN FELLOWSHIP CENTER

ALLEN PORTERFIELD
Pastor   April 14, 1982

Dear Friends:

You have probably wondered what has happened to our dear friend co-laborer
of the Faith Dr. Michael Esses. This letter has been suggested by several
of his friends and former students that became aware I was walking with
him through a very deep valley. They have suggested that I should let all
"Mike's" friends and loved ones know his circumstances.

At the present time Michael is recovering from multiple strokes and heart
disease that had left him close to death. In the words of his physician,
"in the early days of a completed stroke, neither progression nor
ultimate outcome can ever be predicted...The eventual extent of neurologic
recovery depends on his age and general state of health as well as on the
size and site of the infarction, his impaired consciousness, mental
deterioration all suggest a poor prognosis. Complete recovery is
uncommon..." However, God is still and will continue to be a miracle
working God.

Two and one-half years have gone by since Michael left the states under
circumstances which would have broken the "spirit" of most any man.
Finding himself in poor health and emotionally drained Michael was served
with divorce proceedings by Betty. This precipitated the move to Mexico and
the subsequent total breakdown of his health.

Michael is now on the road to recovery. Physically, emotionally and
Spiritually we are seeing the God of Abraham, Isaac, Jacob and the Father
of our Jesus bring reconciliation and restoration. The paralysis, lack of
sight and conscious unawareness are disappearing as our miracle working
God heals Michael.

During the months of critical illness Michael was cared for by a "God sent
nurse, a woman of faith." Michael and "B.J." are now married and have a
beautiful little girl named Deborah. The Scripture indicates that man
does not understand his own heart nor does he consider his own ways. And,
they do sometimes cause heart ache and sorrow. But, God said he would
never leave us nor forsake us. He will even cause our circumstances to
work out for His glory and our good. (Romans 8:28).

Michael needs your prayers and love as God continues His healing process. I'm praying that the Holy Spirit will touch Him in a new and fresh way that Michael has never known.

You may write Michael through my post office box and I'll be pleased to forward it to him without delay.

...in the bond of HIS Love,

Allen Porterfield

P.O. BOX 2639 • COVINA, CA 91722 • PHONE (213) 331-2619

When I read this letter I couldn't believe my eyes. I was getting blamed for the divorce and the total breakdown of Michael's health. After I thought about the contents of Allen's letter, I sat down and composed one of my own:

Mrs. Betty Lee DeBlase
146 So. Trevor Ave.
Anaheim, Ca. 92806

Rev. Alan Porterfield   May 15,1982
P.O. Box 2639
Covina, Ca. 91722

Dear Alan,

I have recently received a copy of the letter you have been sending out for Michael. It is very kind of you to help him, but I feel you are being extremly unfair to me with the way you have written this letter. As a minister you have an obligation not to be bias and give the people the wrong impression.

You have stated in your third paragraph that the reason that Mike left his family for Mexico was that he had been served with divorce papers. Yes, he was served with divorce papers, but you failed to tell the people ,why. You and I both know he left because he had an affair going with his present wife and a child was on the way.

You state that Michael left two and one-half years ago , but you fail to say that the child is two years of age. It doesn't take too much of a mathematician to figure out " B.J.s" condition when they left here. Also the baby things he charged to the charge accounts gave us a clue to his circumstances.

The ironic thing about the reason you give for Mike's departure is that when it behooved him he denied that he even knew that a divorce was pending. (Read exhibit B that Michael submitted to his attorney many months after he left.)

Alan, you are a man of God and I know that you think you are doing the right thing, but certain facts just can't be ignored. The fifth paragraph of your letter is an example. You state that God sent this woman into Mike's life. Well since he was still married and living with me when this event took place and this child was conceived, my only conclusion must be that you think that not only does God condone adultry ,He also must set the situation up.

I couldn't agree with you more that Michael needs
prayer, but that prayer needs to be directed towards his
repentence for the disgrace he brought upon his family and
his God. As long as you and others accept these lies and
refrain from making him face what he has done, Jesus can't
begin to bless him, for my bible tells me that I must make
things right with my fellowman before He will hear my prayers.

Until we received the copy of your letter , we knew about
the child, but we didn't know whether it was a boy or girl. All
Laurie could say was " no wonder my Dad dosn't want me any more,
he has replaced me with another daughter."

Alan, there are deep hurts in my children that will take
alot of time and love to eradicate. Letters like yours do nothing
to heal these wounds. If you really want to look for victims in
this matter , they are much closer to you than New Mexico.

I close now with one request. If you intend to send out
anymore letters in Mike's behalf, please refraim from mention-
ing my name in any form. I refuse to allow any more blame to
be placed upon me for the sins committed by another. It's time
Michael accepted his resposibility for what has happened to
his life. I would hate to have to take this matter further, but
I will if it becomes necessary.

                    In Jesus Name,

I wrote this letter to Allen in May of 1982. In July he called me, asking if he and Pastor Wilkerson could come to see me. I couldn't imagine what these men wanted to see me about. Reluctantly, I said yes. I really wasn't eager to see Ralph Wilkerson, because he had hurt me with his complete desertion of me after Mike had gone. I wasn't too thrilled about seeing Allen, either, after all the trouble he had caused me. I felt betrayed by him.

I called Bob at work and asked him to come home, because I didn't want to see these men alone. When I told Laurie that they were coming, she said she had a few things she wanted to say to them, too. So, when Ralph and Allen arrived, they had to talk to all three of us.

They both said they had come to ask my forgiveness. Ralph, because he had deserted me in my hour of need. Allen, because he hadn't believed me when I told him about Mike.

I'm not sure what Mike did to Allen to finally show his true colors, but apparently it was starting to sink in that Mike was not what Allen had thought he was. Allen told me that he sincerely had believed that Mike was telling him the truth. At that point, I interrupted Allen to say, "Allen, Mike wouldn't know the truth if it jumped on him, but I think you were sincere. I also think you were sincerely wrong."

Allen's support of Mike had cost me thousands of dollars in attorney fees, and had humiliated me by blaming me for the divorce from coast to coast in his letter. He had also allowed Mike to shred my reputation with his lies, here in the same city where my children and I will probably spend the rest of our lives. Yet, looking at the man's face, I knew he would never realize what he had done. The only thing for me to do was forgive him.

When Laurie had her turn to speak, she told both men that her father had gotten away with everything he ever did, no matter how bad or out of line he was, and was never held accountable for his actions. It was in those pastors' power to stop him, but they wouldn't do it. Now she was afraid he was too far gone ever to get back. She started crying and said, "I know I'll never see him on earth again, but I was hoping I was going to see him in heaven."

Laurie is just a young girl, but she knew that it had been the responsibility of these men to chastise her father when he was caught in sin. It wasn't that they didn't know: I had begged for help. She asked them, "Why didn't you set him a good example? Why didn't you take your jobs as shepherds seriously and take care of your sheep?" It wasn't that she was blaming them for Mike's sins, she was blaming them for letting him get away with them.

Most of us, when we see sin, either turn our backs on it, hoping it will go away, or sweep it under the carpet, so we don't have to look at it. Or, we compromise completely and don't even call it sin anymore. We can keep on avoiding reality, but even if we spraypaint it, glue glitter and sequins all over it, or trim it with rick-rack, the Lord is still going to call it sin on judgment day.

When Laurie finished talking, Ralph and I went into my library where we could speak privately. Ralph apologized again for not seeing me for such a long time. He told me the reason he hadn't been in touch with me: Allene. He explained that because I was divorced and then remarried, I became a fallen woman in Allene's eyes. She didn't want her husband to have anything to do with me. He added that it was because of this rigid morality on Allene's part that he "had been in that awkward position for all these years."

I knew Ralph was referring to his affair, which had happened so many years before. I told him, "Ralph, you should have told Allene about that woman from the very beginning. You have spent your life every since this happened compromising yourself one time after another, because of your fear of exposure. I know you tolerated Mike's corruption because you were afraid he would tell Allene. I just wish you could have said, 'Take your best shot, Mike, I've already told my wife.' Then you could have landed on him with both feet, like he deserved."

Ralph acknowledged that what I said was true, but he said, "You just can't imagine how violently Allene would react if she ever found out."

Then Ralph told me a related worry he had. He knew that I knew about the problems he and Paul were having at Melodyland. They were escalating at a rapid rate as both of these men tried to control Melodyland's finances. Ralph voiced his fear that Paul might tell Allene about this secret.

I tried to reassure him by saying, "Ralph, I know Paul well. He is a consumate businessman, and when it comes to battling you about money, he will give you no quarter. But when it comes to revealing your personal business, that is not his style. Paul deals in the boardroom, not the bedroom."

I would never have revealed Ralph's secret here if he hadn't informed me a few months later that he had finally told Allene. I think even he realized it was only a matter of time before she found out, so it was best that he tell her himself.

After the two men left, Bob and I were convinced that a lot of good had happened during our meeting with Allen and Ralph. We took Ralph's later confidence in telling Allene about his affair as part of the benefit of that afternoon, and we were also gratified to learn later that Allen sent another letter to his mailing list, this time stating that he could no longer support Mike's ministry.

The clouds of scandal seemed to be gathering over Melodyland with increasing speed. Ralph's extravagant spending habits were becoming the topic of conversation among congregation members. The persistent rumor that the police were interested in the finances of Melodyland could not be squelched, no matter how much Ralph reassured everyone from the pulpit.

Bob and I awoke one morning to read this startling piece of news over our coffee and toast. Our local newspaper stated that Melodyland Christian Center was suing Paul's Church Managment Inc. (CMI), charging them with usurious business practices. What in the world was Ralph thinking about? Ever since I began at Christian Center, I had heard Ralph state that Christians were not supposed to sue one another. Yet, he was doing exactly what he had preached against. I remembered that even Michael had given me that argument when I filed suit for divorce. He said that it was not right for heathens to decide our property settlement. He felt I should let the pastors decide what my share should be. I told him that we lived in a land that had experts to deal with such matters.

Later that morning I called Paul and asked him what the lawsuit was all about. He told me he was as surprised as I was, because there were no grounds for the suit. I asked Paul to explain it to me.

Paul explained that usury was charging more interest for a loan than the law allows. He said, "This would not apply to us even if we had done it because we did not give Melodyland a loan. It was a purchase lease-back arrangement."

Paul said the ironic thing about the lawsuit was that the attorneys who had filed the suit for Melodyland were the same ones who had written a letter to the board of Melodyland, recommending that they accept CMI's deal in the first place.

When I hung up from Paul I was more confused than ever. What Ralph was doing didn't even make sense. I was not surprised when I found out a few days later that Melodyland had dropped the suit, and Ralph was asking Paul to come back. Shortly after this I contracted a critical infection and underwent emergency major surgery. While I was in the hospital recuperating, Ralph came to see me. After the usual amenities about how I felt, Ralph let me know why he had come to see me. He wanted me to talk to Paul Roper to see if I couldn't get Paul to stop harrassing him about Melodyland's finances. I asked Ralph what Paul was doing and Ralph said Paul was trying to take his church away from him. Pastor admitted that he had made some bad decisions, and he knew that church management was not his expertise, but he said he was not guilty of all the things Paul was accusing him of. I asked him if he was aware of some of the areas in which he had problems. He replied that the only thing he was worried about was his American Express Card. He said he knew that there were personal purchases on the card that Melodyland shouldn't have paid but did.

When I asked Ralph how much he figured he owed on the American Express, he said about $17,000. I said, "Well, Ralph, if that is the extent of your problem, it looks like the answer is fairly simple. Just pay Melodyland what you owe." I guessed from the look on Ralph's face that this was just the tip of the iceberg, but I couldn't say anymore because I didn't know the extent of his complicity.

I knew one other area Paul was pretty upset about. That was the amount of money guest evangelist Dwight Thompson had taken out of Melodyland. Ralph invited Dwight to preach forty different times between March 1981 and September 1982, and Dwight had taken more than $300,000 in offerings. According to the CMI agreement, Ralph was not supposed to let this happen.

Before Ralph left, he asked me to pray for him, which I did. In spite of all that Ralph has done and been accused of, I still love him, and wish God's very best for him. I prayed that the Lord would give him the wisdom to do the right thing for himself, the people, and for Melodyland. I prayed that the Lord would give Ralph the courage to face what must be faced and the strength to endure the unendurable. I knew in my heart that the day of reckoning was at hand for Ralph, not because he was hated, but because he was loved by God. God chastises those who belong to him.

A few weeks later we opened the paper to read this headline: "Pastor of Melodyland Subject of Anaheim Police Investigation." The article related that the probe had been going on for several months and the department in charge of the case dealt only in criminal cases. Ralph was being investigated for fraudulent misuse of funds.

Melodyland was in an uproar. Everyone was taking sides, and the congregation was being split right down the middle. Finally, Ralph agreed to take a ninety day sabbatical from preaching at Melodyland. The day this was announced from the platform at Melodyland, the place came apart at the seams.

A line-up of well-known charismatic leaders began to fill the pulpit at Melodyland to preach in place of Ralph. David Wilkerson, Kenneth Copeland, Mario Murillo, Jerry Savelle, Dick Mills, Jim Bakker, and even Robert Schuller of Garden Grove's famous Crystal Cathedral came to Melodyland during this crisis. One theme ran through the messages of many of these people: "Don't touch the anointed of God."

What these people failed to see was that, if Ralph was guilty of fraudulent misuse of funds, he had put himself under the law of the land. No one, including the clergy, is exempt from the just laws of our country.

I knew the climate was getting ugly at Melodyland, but nothing prepared me for a phone call I received one morning. The man calling me said that the latest gossip sweeping the church was that Paul Roper had raped a young girl. I was terribly dismayed when I heard this, but when the identity of the girl was revealed, my Laurie, and the source of the story, Mike Esses, was traced, I was horrified!

I contacted Paul and told him that this rumor had started. He contacted some of the men at Melodyland and had them backtrack to find its source. They finally narrowed it to one couple, who revealed they had learned the story from a very reliable source: Michael Esses. Mike had told the couple that Paul had raped Laurie and that I wouldn't allow Mike to expose Paul because of my own sexual involvement with Paul.

This was utterly vile. How could this man stoop so low as to take a terrible event like rape and use it in his vendetta against me? No wonder the couple thought Mike was a reliable source. Who would ever imagine that a father would use a tragedy like what had happened to Laurie to further his own perverted goals?

When I talked to Paul the night we found out, he was very subdued. He said, "Betty, for the first time since Mike left, I can truely understand what it has been like for you. It is absolutely devastating to know that there are people out there who are willing to believe these things about you. My God, I would rather be accused of murder than rape!"

Laurie overhead Bob and me talking about this latest situation and her reaction saddened me. I would have preferred that she cried, but her quiet acceptance of the betrayal of her father let me know, louder than words, that she realized she was nothing to her father anymore. I put my arms around my silent daughter and silently asked the question I had asked so many times before: "Michael, Michael, *why?*"

A few days later Laurie and I sat at the kitchen table, sharing cups of coffee. I knew my daughter needed to talk, but I was worried. To tell you the truth, I didn't have any answers for the questions that were on her heart. I was hurt, too. I felt betrayed, too. And worst of all, I would have given anything to have spared Laurie this cruel burden. There was a lot of apprehension on my part when I asked, "Laurie, do you want to talk about this now?" Her reply cut to the heart of the wound with a perception wise for her young years.

"Mom, it's the anger I can't deal with. I'm not an angry person, but I'm so angry deep inside that my own dad could take the worst thing that ever happened to me and use it for such a rotten reason. I don't know if I'll ever be able to forgive him." Her eyes filled with tears as she continued, "Mom, do you understand what I'm saying? He has invaded the deepest part of me. He has made me feel something that will fester in my soul and separate me from God. I don't know if I'll ever be able to deal with it."

I had to trust God for my answer. I knew I didn't have the answers myself, but my Lord had to have the answers. I told her, "Honey, the very fact that you are worried about how you feel tells me that you will be able to deal with this eventually. You're just going to have to realize that only a sick mind would use such a tragedy for his own selfish ends. You have to forgive such a sick mind. Do you remember what Jesus said on the cross about those who crucified him? 'Father, forgive them, for they know not what they do.' "

Laurie was silent for a moment, thinking. Then she answered me, "I guess this is so hard for me because I really thought Dad loved me. I always wondered if he ever loved the rest of the family, but I always thought he loved me for sure." Laurie had just expressed what puzzled me most about this whole ugly mess. Mike had always been devoted to Laurie. He had always treated her like a princess. It was bad enough that he had walked away from her, but this latest episode was beyond comprehension. No wonder my child was so torn up inside and confused.

I tried to shed some light on the bewildering situation by saying, "Laurie, the man is cornered. He is not thinking about the consequences of what he is doing. He isn't thinking about hurting you: he's thinking about saving himself. He thinks his only way out is to discredit me in order to continue in the ministry. Think about what he has said. At least you will be viewed as the victim by anyone who believes his story. On the other hand, what will people think of me? They'll think I'm a mother so perverted that I protect the man who raped my daughter because of my supposed sexual involvement with him.

Laurie, if he could succeed and make this work he would be home free! No one would ever blame him for leaving such a witch of a wife and mother. He would become the martyr and I would become the monster. Don't give him excuses, Laurie, and don't condone what he's done, but forgive him for his sin. He still needs the grace and forgiveness of God as much as any of us. Don't let him have the power over you to interfere with your own relationship to the Lord."

Michael Esses is not the only popular Christian leader whose personal life is a contradiction to the faith he proclaims and teaches. Although he has been the focus of my story, he is not alone in his sin. Because I and my family have been hurt so badly by Mike, I am all too aware of the damage caused by men with spiritual power who lead lives in rebellion to God. If I only cared for me and my family, I would be little better than a bitter ex-wife, no matter how justified my bitterness was. But I care for more than just my family. I care for Christians all over this country who are being manipulated, lied to, coerced, and made to be unknowing pawns in the unethical practices of the men who claim to be their spiritual leaders. I also have a grave concern for the new Christians who are sucked innocently into such games. It is my prayer that my experiences, as related in this book, will be used by many Christians and churches to provide the impetus for change in American churches. If we don't require our leaders to be accountable to the Lord Jesus Christ, we become participants in their sins.

I have no trouble with the honest failures of Christians. We all fall short and the road to perfection is littered with pitfalls, roadblocks, sandtraps, and barriers. The Lord has provided many opportunities for us to grow and learn as repentant Christians.

My trouble is with the few dishonest leaders who prey on their unsuspecting congregations. The scripture tells us that these men will be with us, but that they can be recognized and should be dealt with. We have every right as Christians to expect and demand honesty, integrity, scruples, ethics, and morality from our spiritual leaders. If the shepherd you have chosen to lead you is dishonest, immoral, or a poor steward of your tithes, then you should be looking for another shepherd.

I am not saying we shouldn't have compassion and love toward a pastor who has fallen. None of us is without sin. But a pastor who falls should have the Christian maturity to rectify the situation immediately. He should repent, ask all of the involved parties for forgiveness, and make restitution for the effects of his sin. Grace is no excuse for sin. We must respect a pastor's repentance, but we have every right to test that repentance. For repentance to be complete, restitution, restoration, and reconciliation must be accomplished.

Unfortunately, Christians often fail to test their shepherds. We have grown more and more apathetic about ministries that reflect open sin in their leaders' lives. These "tarnished ministries" should be eliminated from our world and they can be if we fight for what the Bible promises us.

Christians must never forget the price that was paid for us. The "cheap grace" we have allowed to creep into our faith needs to be wiped out by our really understanding the unlimited sacrifice made for us by Jesus Christ.

An experience I witnessed in Norfolk Virginia brought the reality of that sacrifice home to me, and I share it here. I was in the city to appear on the 700 Club and to tape some video teaching tapes for them. The evening before the taping, I was invited to the studio to watch a guest sculptor rehearse. The studio was dark when we arrived, so I stumbled up the stairs to an empty seat and began watching the stage.

A lone pedestal stood in the middle of a spotlight. There was a mound of clay on top of the turntable, and as music began to swell through the studio, the sculptor stepped out of the surrounding darkness. Reverently, he laid his hands on the soft clay. Slowly and expertly he began to mold the head of Christ. His fingers moved so quickly and with such precision that it seemed only moments before the features began to take shape. The beautiful face of Jesus was created by the loving hands of the sculptor. Softly, in perfect rhythm with the music, the man began to narrate the life of Jesus.

The music grew more intense, and the tone of the sculptor changed, as he narrated the trial of Christ. Suddenly, the sculptor became the prosecutor of Jesus and began to berate and harrange him. He mocked him, "Here's your scepter, you King of the Jews!" He shoved a stick alongside Christ's head. Then he spit in the face of Jesus and said, "Here's your mantle", as he draped a piece of purple cloth around the shoulders, with a derisive toss. The mute face of the molded Christ was the perfect example of the silent Jesus in the face of his accusers.

The music took on an even more discordant note, as the sculptor grabbed a whip and began to scourge the head of Jesus. "WHERE IS YOUR GOD TO SAVE YOU NOW?" he shouted, as the features of Christ began to distort from the repeated blows on the damp clay.

Quickly, the sculptor snatched up some strips of clay and slammed them into the forehead of Jesus, and he began to form the crown of thorns. Slowly and deliberately he plucked out the cruel thorns that pierced the head of my Jesus. Scarlet blood suddenly appeared on the forehead and began to course down the mangled face of my Lord.

The music softened now and the voice of the sculptor lost its harshness and an infinite sadness seemed to envelope the surroundings. There was a moment of silence, and then the anguished voice of the sculptor echoed Christ's words: "My God, why hast thou forsaken me?"

Sitting in my seat, in the empty and dark studio, I was transported back to the time of Christ. I was brought face to face with the reality of the price that had been paid by Christ for me. I had always accepted the fact that Jesus had died for me, but tonight I understood the magnitude of that sacrifice.

My body was racked with sobs as I thought of the Father watching his Son die. I have lost a son, and I know what agony it is. But I also know I would never have had the strength to lay my Donnie on the altar and deliberately sacrifice him, not only for those who loved, but even for my enemies. God the Father made this sacrifice, and Jesus, his Son, went willingly to the cross for you and me.

This sacrifice deserves our best from us. We have to mold our lives to reflect our commitment to Jesus Christ. The Father's sacrifice of his Son was so pure and complete that we can't permit ministries that are corrupt to flourish in his name. This is not just God's problem. It is our problem, and we need to face this fact. We are the Lord's ambassadors on this earth, and he wants us to assume our responsibilities. If we refuse to compromise, if we insist on righteousness, then the "tarnished ministries" can become things of the past.

How Long Will It Go On?

In the last three years many well-meaning Christians have told me that "'Mike is a repentant man," or "Mike is living a repentant life." How my heart would rejoice if I actually were presented evidence that Mike is repentant! You can't live with and love a man for twenty-eight years without continuing to hope that somehow, sometime, he will get his life straightened out. And you can't experience the unconditional love and forgiveness of Jesus Christ in your own life without desiring that same sort of relationship for someone to whom you were so close for so long. I can't think of many prayers Bob and I pray more fervently or more often than our prayer that Michael would truly repent and turn to the Lord.

Unfortunately, there are no signs that Mike has made a true and biblical repentance. While some Christians have been in the midst of assuring us of Michael's repentance, others have relayed to us hard evidence that Mike still operates as he has always operated, still lies about himself and his background, still hungers after more and more wealth, and still dishonors the Lord in whose name he claims to minister.

I can't be bitter at Mike. He has patterned his life in this way and I seriously doubt if now he has the inner strength to stop this life of sin and turn to the Lord on his own. He needs the strong intervention of Christians who can work with the Holy Spirit in compelling him to change. I pray for Christians to be strong enough to confront Mike (and there are thousands of "Mikes" in this Christian world) and be partners in the Holy Spirit's purifying work. Unfortunately, most Christians who find out about the *real* Mike just retreat and say, "Well let the Lord deal with him. We don't want to cause dissension." Do you know what people like this are doing? They are refusing to take their Christian responsibility to help their fellow Christians *no matter what state they are in.* It's no friend who only helps you when everything is going great! It takes real courage and faith in the Lord to be willing to call a Christian to task, to point out his sin, and to exhort him to repentance. When will a church Mike is at ever have the courage to do what the Bible says, strengthening themselves, as well as saving Mike from his own sinful compulsions?

Mike has been busy during the three years since he left here. He and his new wife, B.J., have a daughter who was conceived while Mike and I were still together, Mike left here with hundreds of thousands of dollars in assets, although, as we have seen, he told everyone his divorce left him penniless. He tells similar stories today, in his new home in Clovis, New Mexico.

We first found out that Mike had moved to Clovis from a friend, who had recently had a long conversation with the head of the Full Gospel Businessmen's Association in Clovis. This man was excited that Michael Esses and his family were moving to town to start a school and were taking over a church just outside town. The leader was excited that Clovis had the honor of obtaining the famous ex-rabbi and scholar, Michael Esses. The leader told of the beautiful new home Mike had purchased in Clovis, and of how, when Mike and he had gone to the bank to arrange the mortgage, Mike had so little business sense that he didn't know what collateral was! When the term was explained to him, Mike responded that he had a little bit of jewelry, but didn't know if it was worth any more than $15,000. The appraised value turned out to be $60,000. The Clovis man remarked, "What a man of faith! He doesn't even know anything about finances!"

This from the same Mike Esses who spent most of his adult life transacting more financial business than two average men together! The same Mike Esses who manipulated Allen Porterfield and his congregation into paying all of his attorney's fees, and on a visit to these same people a year ago, claimed he was living on stale bread and moldy cheese and was forced to sleep on the floor for lack of a bed. The same Mike Esses who claimed to be penniless, dependent on an old Jewish couple to nurse him back to health, and who didn't have enough money for food, while in reality he was living quite comfortably with his new wife and child.

After we found out Mike was in Clovis, long-time friend and former Melodyland employee Lowell Jones called this Clovis businessman and tried to fill him in on Mike's real past. Lowell told the man that Michael was not a rabbi and that his credentials were phony. He told the man how Michael had left his family and taken a small fortune with him. Lowell's call was in vain. Mike had warned the people in Clovis, supposedly telling them that Satan didn't like his ministry and would use lots of people from his past to try to cause trouble for him. The Full Gospel Businessman believed Mike. I guess he never stopped to think that maybe Satan had nothing to do with Mike's trouble, that perhaps these "bad things" were a result of Mike's sinful past.

Lowell Jones also talked with the pastor of a church in Las Cruces, New Mexico, where Mike had ministered for some time before moving to Clovis. Mike had taught a Wednesday night class at this minister's church. The pastor told Lowell he had been suspicious of Mike, but hadn't wanted to pry because his congregation liked Mike so much. He was glad when Mike decided to relocate in Clovis.

After Lowell shared Mike's past with the pastor, the man related that he had taken up a collection of over $2,400 from his congregation for Mike. Frustrated, he said, "Now I don't even know why I did it for him!" Lowell responded, "Don't feel too bad, Brother, you can't imagine how many collections I took up for Mike at Melodyland before I knew Mike's income was more than I could ever dream of!" Unfortunately, this pastor in Las Cruces declined to help us warn people in Clovis. His wife related that they were just glad Mike was leaving them alone, and that they didn't want to offend Mike's new father-in-law, an influential and wealthy Full Gospel Businessman with whom they had some relationship.

After this we sent our investigators to New Mexico. Their first stop was in Alamogordo, where Mike had spent some time at a local church speaking. The church staff and pastor welcomed our investigators' evidence concerning Mike, because it gave them confirmation of their recently made decision not to invite Mike back to their church and not to endorse his ministry. This is an example of responsible pastoring of a congregation, and the people of Christ Community Church in Alamogordo should be proud of their pastor, who based his decision initially on Mike's inconsistent walk, even though he was unaware of the vast extent of Mike's duplicity. In Alamogordo the investigators were also able to obtain several of Mike's testimony and teaching tapes for research. As you will see below, Mike himself has confirmed by his words that he is not repentant and is perpetuating lies just as he did throughout his ministry at Melodyland.

The team's first stop in Clovis was to see Pastor Roy Denton of Parkland Baptist Church. One of the team is a licensed Baptist minister, so he felt he would have some rapport with Pastor Denton. In their meeting the pastor was shown ample documentation of Mike's duplicity and sinful activities. (Many of these documents are reproduced in the appendix.) Pastor Denton was shocked that Mike had been ordained by the Southern Baptist church in California. His remark was: "This is the most unorthodox Baptist ordination I have ever seen!"

Providentially, a meeting had already been scheduled with the other Clovis Baptist ministers. At this meeting Pastor Denton exposed Michael Esses to his fellow pastors. With the other Baptist pastors warned, Pastor Denton took care of his own flock by informing his own congregation, from the pulpit on Sunday morning, to steer clear of Michael Esses because of his documented personal and credibility problems. This pastor is a strong biblical leader. He took the difficult responsibility of speaking the truth to protect other congregations and his own flock, even though he was exposing himself to criticism by others. Problems like this are not dealt with by sweeping them under the rug. There should be more pastors like Denton, who will stand up publicly for their convictions.

Mike appears to be doing well in Clovis right now. He lives in a $137,000 house when the average home in Clovis is valued at only $40,000. He put down $32,000 to make the purchase. And yet he contacted old friends and relatives (such as his niece), to send him money since he was penniless. This "penniless" man drives a 1983 Cadillac and a new Buick.

According to a Clovis newspaper article, the land and school facilities, worth several hundred thousand dollars, were donated to Mike. When the team returned from New Mexico, they delivered to me ten tapes of Mike's teachings and testimonies. Mike is continuing to lie, to cover up, and to pretend he's something he is not. Below is a brief portion of my analysis of his taped claims:

I. Michael claims in his current testimony that his family has lived in Allepo, Syria for the last 2000 years. *FACT:* Michael's father and mother were both born in Egypt.

2. Michael states his father's self-made fortune was 30 million dollars. *FACT:* At his death, his father's estate was divided evenly among his brothers. Michael received $55,000, making his father's estate around $250,000.

3. He states his knuckles were broken numerous times as a from of discipline by his parents and rabbis (teachers). *FACT:* He had no broken knuckles during the time I knew him, and family members consistently deny that his parents and teachers abused him and that instead they were fair, kind, and decent.

4. Michael states that he wore two curls of hair over his ears in accordance with his strict Jewish faith. *FACT:* Only Hasidic Jews wear earlocks. Michael was never a Hasidic Jew.

5. Michael states he enlisted in the Air Corps the day after Pearl Harbor, December 7, 1941, was a gunnery instructor, stayed in the service for three and one-half years, and was discharged an officer. *FACT:* He enlisted on November 24, 1942. He went to radio operator and mechanic school. He was in the service for only six months and two days. He was discharged at his highest grade, Private First Class. (See the copy of his discharge papers in the appendix.)

6. He says he returned to the Yeshiva to continue his rabbinical training after his service duty. *FACT:* Michael was released from the service May 25, 1943. He was married the next day to Elizabeth Magni in St. Louis. During the next few years, instead of going to school as claimed, Michael was busy fathering and supporting four children. In September of 1948 he moved his family to California. I have spoken to the first Mrs. Esses and she

was gracious enough to send me a copy of her marriage certificate (see appendix). She also informed me that Michael has twelve grandchildren ranging in age from two to sixteen years.

7. Michael states he was ordained a rabbi on June 30, 1950, in New York City. At the same time he received his doctorate in Hebrew Letters. *FACT:* Michael was already living in California in 1950. As we recounted earlier in the book, Mike fabricated his ordination and his doctorate of Hebrew Letters.

8. Michael states that he was ordained a Presbyterian minister. *FACT:* Michael was never ordained by the Presbyterians. He never had the education or the training and was never considered by any Presbyterian ordination board.

9. Michael asserts that he joined Pastor Ralph Wilkerson's staff in 1963, and taught at Melodyland for 16 years, until 1979. *FACT:* Michael was not even a Christian in 1963. He claimed his salvation in 1965, and we were members of the Presbyterian Church from 1965 through 1968. Mike taught at Melodyland just over 10 years.

10. Michael states he has been a personal counselor to such world leaders as Sadat, Begin, Reagan, Carter, and Nixon. He says he spent a week with Sadat at his palace in Aswan. *FACT:* While Mike and I were together, he never even met these men. He has never been in Egypt. He has had little opportunity to form these relationships since he left me in 1979. According to him, during the years since he left, he was bedridden, paralyzed, and blind from strokes.

11. Michael states on one tape (Clovis, January 15, 1983) that he suffered four strokes. On another tape (Alamogordo, January 23, 1983) he stated he had eleven strokes.

12. Michael states he had just received a call from his niece. She had the good news that his orthodox Jewish family had decided to welcome him back into the family. They had held a mock funeral for him and buried his coffin when he converted to Christianity, but now they were relenting. His brother read *Michael, Michael,* held a family council, his coffin was exhumed, and he was once more part of the family! *FACT:* Michael's family testifies that they never held a funeral for him. His niece

said, "My father was the last of Michael's brothers alive, and he died six years ago."

The investigators returned with 10 tapes. The above are only twelve of the typical lies Mike peppered all the tapes with. I could continue for pages refuting them, point by point. What really matters is that the tapes are evidence that Mike is *not* a repentant man, and he is *not* living a repentant life.

My earnest prayer is that Mike will get the intervention he needs and come to a true repentance. I also pray that Christians everywhere will take their God-given responsibilities seriously, and stand for the truth in matters like this even if it is embarrassing and even if it hurts. Michael and hundreds of Christian leaders like him succeed in their deceit because Christians let them. Don't let them. Love them enough to save them from themselves. I pray that God the Holy Spirit will touch Michael's heart and do the work necessary to turn a testimony of lies into a testimony of truth.

Appendix

ENLISTED RECORD OF

Esses	Max	(None)	15339394	Private 1cl,
(Last name)	(First name)	(Middle initial)	(Army serial number)	

Born in .... **Brooklyn** ...., in the State of .... **New York**

Enlisted .... **November 24**, 19 **42**, at **Fort Thomas, Kentucky**

When enlisted or inducted he was .... **19 6/12** .... years of age and by occupation

a .. **Aircraft Mechanic** ....

He had .. **Brown** .... eyes, ... **Black** .... hair, ... **Ruddy** .... complexion

and was .... **5** .... feet .... **7** .... inches in height.

Completed .... **0** .... years, ... **6** .... months, .. **2** .. days service for longevity pay

Prior service: ² .. **None**

Noncommissioned officer .... **None**

Military qualifications ³ .... **None**

Army specialty .... **Student**

Attendance at **Radio Operator and Mechanic School, Scott Field, Illinois.**
(Name of noncommissioned officers' or special service school)

Battles, engagements, skirmishes, expeditions .... **None** ....

Certification made for mustering-out payment in the amount of $200

Decorations, service medals, citations .... **None** ....

Wounds received in service .... **None**

Date and result of smallpox vaccination ⁴ .... **11-25-42 Vaccinia**

Date of completion of all typhoid-paratyphoid vaccinations ⁴ **12-30-42**

Date and result of diphtheria immunity test (Schick) ⁴ .... **None**

Date of other vaccinations (specify vaccine used) .... **None**

Physical condition when discharged .... **Fair** .... Married or single .. **Single**

Honorably discharged by reason of ⁵ .. **Section II, AR 615-360**

Character .. *Very Good* .. Periods of active duty ⁶ Fr **11-24-42 to 5-25-43**

Remarks ⁷ **Time lost under the 107th AW 25 days. Fr 4-23-43 to 5-17-43 incl (WLD-EPTS)**
Soldier entitled to travel pay to Cincinnati, Ohio.

Print of Right Thumb

```
FINANCE OFFICE
SCOTT FIELD, ILL
DATE May 25, 1943
PAID IN FULL THIS
DATE $ 59.20
TO INCLUDE TRAVEL
PAY TO Cincinnati, Ohio
          W. C. Hawke
W. C. HAWKE, Lt. C.I., U.S.
```

Signature of soldier — *Max Esses*

ROBERT W. SUCKOW, 1st Lt., Air Corps,
Unit Personnel Officer.

INSTRUCTIONS FOR ENLISTED RECORD

¹ Enter date of induction only in case of trainee inducted under Selective Training and Service Act of 1940 (Bull. 25, W. D., 1940), in all other cases enter date of enlistment. Eliminate word not applicable.

² For each enlistment give company, regiment, or arm or service with inclusive dates of service, grade, cause of discharge, number of days lost under AW 107 if none, so state), and number of days retained and cause of retention in service for convenience of the Government, if any.

³ Enter qualifications in arms, horsemanship, etc. Show the qualification, date thereof, and number, date, and source of order announcing same.

⁴ See paragraph 12, AR 40-210.

⁵ If discharged prior to expiration of service, give number, date, and source of order or full description of authority therefor

⁶ Enter periods of active duty of enlisted men of the Regular Army Reserve and the Enlisted Reserve Corps and dates of induction into Federal service in the cases of members of the National Guard.

⁷ In all cases of men who are entitled to receive Certificates of Service under AR 615-360, enter here appointments and ratings held and all other items of special proficiency or merit other than those shown above.

INSTRUCTIONS FOR CERTIFICATE OF DISCHARGE

AR 345-470.

Insert name: as, "John J. Doe," in center of form.

Insert Army serial number, grade, company, regiment, or arm of service; as "18361812"; "Corporal, Company A, 1st Infantry"; "Sergeant, Quartermaster Corps."
The name and grade of the officer signing the certificate will be typewritten or printed below the signature.

☆ U. S. GOVERNMENT PRINTING OFFICE : 1943 O

E MORELAND
CAP
ISSUING OFF

Michael's discharge papers, which shows the duration of service and his rank when dischaged.

Michael's Marriage license for his first marriage.

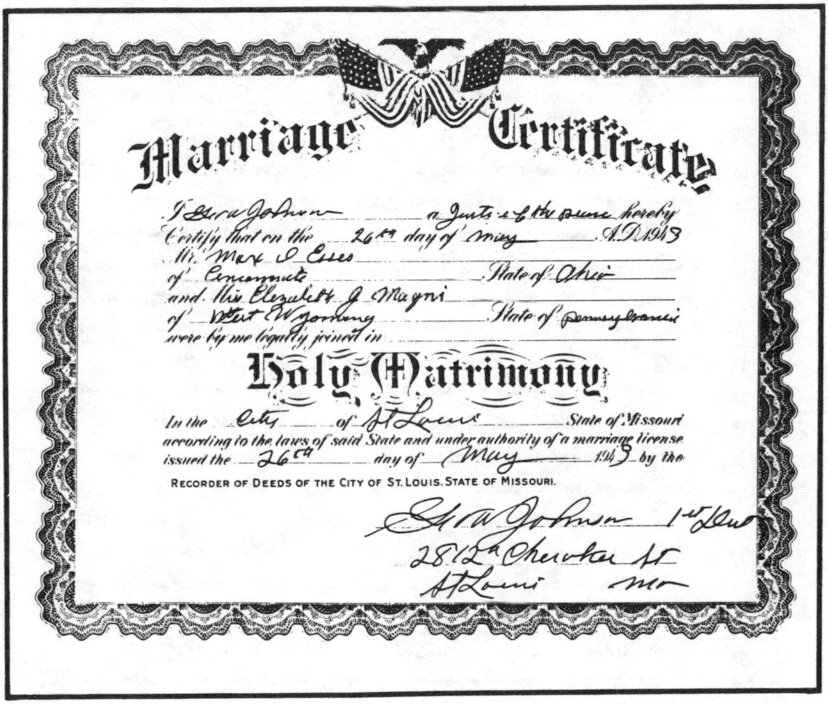

Marriage Certificate

I Geo. W. Johnson a Justice of the Peace hereby
Certify that on the 26th day of May A.D. 1943
Mr. Max I. Esses
of Cincinnati State of Ohio
and Miss Elizabeth J. Magni
of West Wyoming State of Pennsylvania
were by me legally joined in

Holy Matrimony

In the City of St Louis State of Missouri
according to the laws of said State and under authority of a marriage license
issued the 26th day of May 1943 by the
RECORDER OF DEEDS OF THE CITY OF ST. LOUIS. STATE OF MISSOURI.

Geo W. Johnson 1st Dist
2812a Cherokee St
St Louis Mo

Michael's divorce papers, granted a year after our marriage.

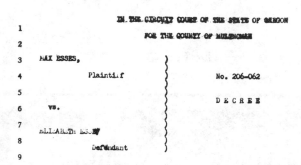

IN THE CIRCUIT COURT OF THE STATE OF OREGON

FOR THE COUNTY OF MULTNOMAH

MAX ESSES,

        Plaintiff   )   No. 206-062

vs.   )   D E C R E E

ELIZABETH ESSES

        Defendant   )

Now at this time this matter coming on to be heard, the plaintiff
appearing by and through his attorney THOMAS H. RYAN, of RYAN AND PELAY,
the defendant appearing not, and the State of Oregon appearing by and through
a duly appointed and qualified Deputy District Attorney for Multnomah County,
Oregon; and it appearing that the defendant did not answer or interpose any
defense herein and did not controvert the allegations of plaintiff's complaint
or any part thereof and that the defendant is now in default herein, which
said default has been duly and regularly entered herein; and the Court after
hearing the testimony being of the opinion that the plaintiff is entitled to
a decree of divorce from the defendant; and that the defendant shall have
care, custody, and control of the minor children of the parties hereto, to-wit,
JUDITH EILEEN, aged eight; AUDRY GALE, aged six; TERRIE LYNN, aged four; DAVID
STARK, aged two, and that the plaintiff will pay to the defendant for support
of said children the sum of $37.50 per month for each child of the parties hereto,
and the property settlement agreement of the parties herein is approved.

NOW THEREFORE, BASED UPON THE TESTIMONY GIVEN, IT IS HEREBY ORDERED,
ADJUDGED AND DECREED that the bonds of matrimony heretofore and now existing
between the plaintiff, MAX ESSES, and the defendant , ELIZABETH ESSES, herein
be and they are hereby dissolved and that the plaintiff be and he hereby is granted
a decree of divorce from the defendant herein, and further, that the plaintiff
is to pay the defendant the sum of $37.50 a month for the support and maintenance of
each of the minor children of the parties hereto, to-wit: JUDITH EILEEN, aged
eight; AUDRY GALE, aged six; TERRIE LYNN, aged four; DAVID STARK, aged two,
and that the defendant shall have care, custody, and control of the minor children

Page

1 - Decree

RYAN & PELAY
ATTORNEYS AT LAW
EQUITABLE BUILDING
PORTLAND 4, OREGON

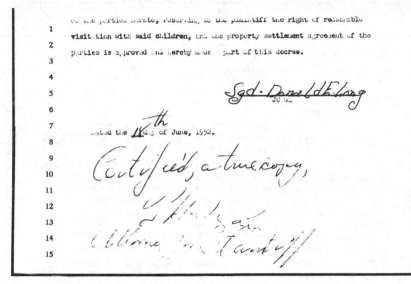

1   of the parties hereto, reserving to the plaintiff the right of reasonable
2   visitation with said children, and the property settlement agreement of the
3   parties is approved and hereby made part of this decree.
4
5   *Sgd. Donald E. Long*
6   JUDGE
7   Dated the 18th day of June, 1952.
8
9   *Certified, a true copy,*
10
11
12
13   *J. H. Bain*
14   *Attorney for plaintiff*
15

This Certifies
that

May Eases
of Portland
Province of Oregon, U. SA.
~~Dominion of Canada~~

and

Betty Lee Neal
of Portland
Province of Oregon, U.S.A.
~~Dominion of Canada~~

were united by me in the Bonds of

Holy Matrimony

on the 27th day of October 1951
at St Andrew's Presbyterian Church, Victoria BC

Lewis O. McLean
Minister

Witnesses
Charlotte E Klapproth
Frances D. McLean

License Number 38203-C

Our first marriage license, issued one year before Michael obtained a divorce from his first wife.

Wᵐ A. (Bill) DuMas
Tax and Investment Consultant

Complete Computerized Financial Reporting

May 1,1981

Dear Mr. Rosen,

During our telephone conversation last week you
asked me to send you a statement concerning my knowledge of the
personal and business affairs of Michael and Betty Esses.

In my capacity as accountant for the Esses for the
past several years I have come to know them quite well, not only
in their financial life but also in their personal life. In fact
I was one of the people, much to my regret, that convinced Betty
to return to Michael, after she filed suit against him the first
time. Michael told me he was going to mend his ways. He said that
if Betty would return to him that he would make his family happy.
It wasn't long before we all knew we had been lied to,once again.

That is my first and foremost opinion of Michael
Esses. He is a chronic liar to the point that I'm not sure that
he knows what the truth is half the time.The only criterion he
seems to have for truth is whether it behooves him or not.

Michael has given me many reasons to be suspicious
of his financial matters. One of the main reasons was that he was
so secretive, especially with his wife. She was kept in total ig-
norance concerning his finances. He did not hid the fact that
he didn't want her to know a thing about his business.

Many different times, during the last few years
Michael mentioned to me that he had a third $100,000.00 treasury
note that his wife did not know about. He was forced to tell me
because he knew he would eventually have to report it on his income tax. Since Betty was never consulted about their income tax,
Michael was able to get away without telling her, what he reported.

1742 W. Katella Avenue, Suite 6-A

Orange, California 92667   (714)771-1540

"In All Circumstances • Praise The Lord"

**Letter from our accountant with his knowledgeable assessment of Michael's
financial manipulations.**

I was also made aware that he was cashing checks given to
him as ministry gifts, which he would then hid so they wouldn't go
through his bank account. I can only assume that he was planning
the move that he made in Oct. of 79, namely the abandonment of his
family. He apparantly wanted to leave with as much cash and securities as he could gather togather.

I would imagine he had these securities and cash and gold
secreted in his personal safety deposit box.

My own opinion of Michael Esses, as a man, has been formed
over the years observing him in his business dealings with people
and friends, his relationship with his wife and his children, and
his following at the church.

Michael is a man who seems void of any conscience. He would
preach the word of God out of the same mouth that could utter the
most foul language it has ever been my misfortune to hear from another man, much less a minister.

In attending his classes, at Melodyland, I have observed
him use the most flagrant means to solicit money from his follow-
ers. At one time, he told the people that his retarded child would
not be able to continue her special school, because of prop. 13.
He began to collect money for this need, and the child was still in
school.

Michael's relationship with his wife was a total disaster.
He treated her like a chattel, with absolutely no rights. When I
was working towards their reconciliation, Michael told Betty he
had been living with another woman, in front of me.

His relationship with his children was profoundly damaging,
especially to his son, John. This young man is having a hard time
understanding the hypocrisy his father represents. In short Michael
is not a man a son could admire, much less emulate.

Mr. Rosen if I can be of any other help, please don't
hesitate to call, at any time.

Sincerely,

Bill Dumas

Page 6   The Oracle

Focus on Faith

By Jay Martin

May-June 1983

God can heal your hurt

This month in Focus On Faith, we're blessed to feature an interview with Dr. Michael Esses. Dr. Esses has traveled and ministered the Word of God world-wide in Full Gospel businessmen's conventions and seminars. He has authored seven books, including his testimony, "Michael Michael, Why Do You Hate Me?"

Several months ago he came to Clovis to speak at a Full Gospel Businessmen's banquet. At that time, the Lord spoke to him and directed him to open a Bible school in Clovis called "The Gospel School of the Prophets" — that would open it's arms wide to believers from all denominations.

The land and school facilities, worth several hundred thousand dollars were donated to Dr. Esses, and classes have already begun. The school is west of Clovis on Highway 60-70-84. Dr. Esses leads in a praise and teaching service Sunday afternoons at 1:30 and teaches Hebrew Monday and Tuesday nights at seven. He also has a 5-minute radio program called "Life In The Spirit" on KIJN in Farwell, Texas. For more information, call Dr. Esses at 505-763-3656.

FOF: Dr. Esses, I'd like to take this opportunity to let our readers get to know you. Can you give us a look at your background? We understand you were raised to be a Jewish rabbi.

ESS: Yes I was. I was put in Hebrew school at the age of two, to follow in the footsteps of my ancestors to be a rabbi as they have been for hundreds of years.

We (my ancestors) went into the captivity in Babylon, and then when we returned with Zerrubabel, my family stayed in Jerusalem for awhile, and then migrated to a city in the northern part of Syria. That's where they lived for a couple of thousand years. And then, finally in 1902, my father came to the United States of America.

He was a man who loved God very dearly. He never knew Jesus Christ, but I do know for a fact that I do know Jesus Christ, and I can say unequivically that Jesus is my Lord, and that there's no way to heaven except through Jesus Christ.

FOF: So, He's your Messiah?

That's right. He's my Messiah, my Savior, my healer, my redeemer.

My father honored the principles that God showed him in the Old Testament. He arrived in the lower east side of New York, got himself some wood and built a push cart. Even though he was a chief rabbi, he had to make a living so he bought and sold and traded whatever he could. He would then give his tithe to the Lord daily.

Our God is just, fair and holy. He will always honor His principles. Even though this man did not know Jesus, God honored His principles — in a short 20 years, father was the possessor of 30 million dollars.

FOF: So if you work the Word, the Word will work for you.

ESS: That's right! Absolutely. So, I began studying at Hebrew school at the age of two, and studied for the next 26 years to be ordained a rabbi. I received my doctorate of Hebrew law, and was ordained a rabbi in 1950.

Father prayed and received a message from the Lord that I was to go to California. I got on a train and moved to California. I never actually got a congregation or a synogogue started because I had to earn a living.

Upon arrival in California, I got a job working in a gift shop, then moved into the parking lot business. Then I found myself in the interior decorating business, and from that point on, things went from bad to worse.

You see, I was holding a grudge against God, because my mother died of a heart attack on my seventeenth birthday. As my brother was coming out to California to see me, he was killed outside El Paso in an automobile accident, so I blamed God for all these things.

FOF: This is the returning messiah, the eternal hope of the Jews. Michael, how do you describe your feelings of knowing Jesus as your Messiah after rejecting Him all those many years?

ESS: The only way I can describe he feeling is by my own experience. One minute I was full of bitterness and despair. The next moment, here is the savior of the world standing at my bedside. He loved me so much that He called me by name. Until this day, I'll never forget His voice.

That minute I realized who He was, and fell to my knees and I was filled with that peace I had searched for my entire lifetime. I was filled with a love for myself and my fellow man. I was filled with an understanding that Jesus accomplished everything for me. I understood that from this point on, all I have to do is believe in Him, trust and follow Him and show myself approved.

I joined the church. I met Pastor Ralph Wilkerson of Melodyland School of Theology in Anaheim California. I joined his staff and started teaching Old Testament. I went to the Presbyterian Lay Academy for four years and studied New Testament, then began teaching it.

I praise God that in 1975, I received my PhD in theology from California Western University. I now had a Bachelor of Arts, a Masters of Arts, a doctorate of Hebrew law, a PhD, But these really amounted to nothing. There are really only two degrees that God ever desires a BA and SF — born-again and spirit-filled.

A condensed version of an article in a New Mexico paper which confirms that Michael is still claiming to be a rabbi.